Letters from Isohe

Letters from Isohe

Life on the edge in a
school in South Sudan

ELIZABETH HODGKIN

City *of* Words

Published 2022 by City of Words Ltd, London, UK
www.cityofwords.net

Edited by John Ryle
Design and typography by Lindsay Nash

Photographs on front cover and back cover and in text © John Ryle;
except those on page 32 © Elizabeth Hodgkin, pages 44, 74, 94 ©
Javier Sauras, and page 88 © Brett Morton (courtesy of AVSI, the
Association of Volunteers in International Service www.avsi.org).

Base map courtesy of Freeworld maps (www.freeworldmaps.net)

Print and digital copies of this book may be purchased from
Amazon and other online retailers. Trade enquiries to sales@
cityofwords.net

Editorial enquiries to editorial@cityofwords.net

To support a student in South Sudan contact Opportunity Through
Education (UK Registered Charity Number 1179046) E-mail: alion@
btinternet.com

A CIP record for this book is available from the British Library

ISBN 978-1-9160783-2-1

Contents

ELIZABETH HODGKIN

Elizabeth Hodgkin was a lecturer in the History Department at the University of Khartoum from 1968 to 1973, and a human rights researcher for Amnesty International from 1989 to 2009, reporting on the Middle East and Africa. From February 2012 to December 2013 she taught at St Augustine's School in the village of Isohe, in Imatong State, Eastern Equatoria, South Sudan.

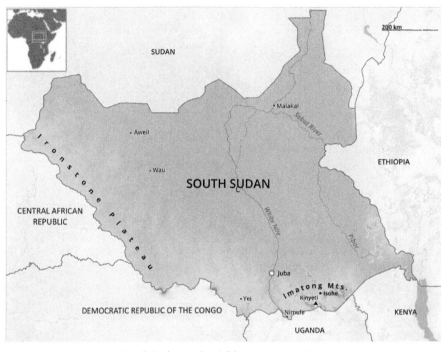

South Sudan and neighbouring countries

St Theresa's Church, Isohe, and the Dongotono Mountains.

Introduction

In 2011, at the age of 70, I decided to go and teach in a secondary school in a remote part of South Sudan. I had retired from my job as an Amnesty International researcher two years before, and decided that I should try to end my working life as I had begun it, as a school teacher in Africa. Half a century earlier I had travelled in various parts of the continent with my father, Thomas Hodgkin, a writer and historian. His style was low-key: arriving in a town he would select the most run-down hotel to stay in; and he generally used the most modest means available of getting from place to place – travelling third class only if fourth was not available. This early acquaintance with ordinary life in African countries encouraged my belief that a new post-colonial world could, as George Canning said of the independence movements in South America, "redress the balance of the old". For me that meant the hope that the emergence of independent states in Africa would break the global stranglehold of the East-West Cold War. This did not come to pass in the way I hoped; but my love of Africa endured.

Between 1964 and 1967 I taught at Kasama Girls' Secondary School in Zambia, just after independence. When, more than forty years later, I decided to return to the field of education, I resolved, without much deep thought, to go to South Sudan.

It had recently gained independence from the northern part of the country after fifty years of intermittent conflict and was said to rank lowest in the world in terms of access to education, so I thought I might be of use there. I had been given a phone number for Sister Rose, a South Sudanese nun from the Sacred Heart Order, who was studying for a Master's in Education in Nairobi, so I called her and she agreed to discuss the possibility. Sister Rose introduced me to Sister Paskwina, founder and head of a primary school in a Catholic mission centre in Eastern Equatoria, the most mountainous part of South Sudan, near the Uganda border. It didn't seem to matter that I wasn't a Catholic. Sister Paskwina invited me to come and teach in Isohe at the primary school she ran there; I said I thought I might be more suited to teaching in a secondary school.

"Well we have St Augustine's too," said Sister Paskwina. "That's our secondary school. You could teach there."

And so it happened that I went to teach in Isohe, at St Augustine's School, for the following two years.

The academic year in South Sudan starts in February. I left for South Sudan towards the end of January. I was aiming to travel in the style my father favoured – by the most economical means and the most direct route – through Kitgum, in Uganda, avoiding airports and capital cities. For bureaucratic reasons, however, I found I had to go first to Juba, capital of South Sudan. I took a bus there from Nairobi, a two-day journey. Then, after some days in Juba, I stopped for another day in Torit, the seat of the Catholic diocese. Finally, seven days after leaving Nairobi, I arrived in Isohe.

I had been expecting something like a displaced camp, with thousands of children under trees, but St Augustine's Secondary School and St Kizito's Primary School were old-established institutions, part of a mission station established by Italians in 1924 in a precipitous valley among steep green, conical mountains. There was a beautiful, tall, Italianate Church, constructed and decorated with frescos after a fire destroyed the old mud-brick church in 1948. The buildings of the secondary school dated from 1950s. Below them were the newer primary school buildings and St Theresa's Hospital, surrounded by tukuls – round mud-brick huts with straw roofs. Opposite the church was a compound where the fathers' house and guest rooms were. Here I was to live for the next two years. There was a football pitch, and a market with a couple of bars and a few shops, some selling foodstuffs, others second-hand clothes and shoes, along with pens (and, unreliably, notebooks), and creams for skin-lightening and hair-blackening. Along the road from the primary school leading north out of the village women sold cassava and greens.

Sister Rose, whose kindness had directed me to Isohe, was an Acholi, and I had somehow assumed that Isohe was in an Acholi-speaking area. I had even equipped myself with an Acholi dictionary. But I found out that the principal languages spoken in the area were Dongotono and Logir, which are closer to Lotuho, the language of one of the principal ethnic groups in Eastern Equatoria. The valley where Isohe is situated rises steeply to a high plateau, the Dito Plateau, and many Dongotono communities live scattered in the mountains around, in villages that cling to the rocks. Below, in the foothills, the Dongotono villages alternate with those of the Logir people; meanwhile there are Lotuho villages north-west of Isohe, and to the south, Lango communities such as the Lokwa, who speak yet another variant of Lotuho.

Sister Paskwina – herself a Logir from a village near Isohe – told me that when she was young buffalo and elephant had roamed in the valley. There are none now, though there are monkeys and duikers to be seen, and, on rare occasions, a leopard. Another of the sisters, Sister Theresina, compared the valley to a hall with a single door for exit and entrance. She had left it for the first time when she was fourteen, she said. It was not till then that she realised she had been living in the most beautiful place in the world.

In the 1960s and 1970s, during the first civil war in South Sudan, these mountains were a refuge for Anyanya rebels (the name means "snake venom" in the language of the Madi, another Equatorian people). Joseph Oduho, a Lotuho who was a senior figure in the movement, was based on the Dito plateau for a time; the old Anyanya base is still visible there. During the second civil war, in the early 1990s when John Garang and his followers had to leave Ethiopia after the fall of Mengistu, the school buildings at Isohe were appropriated as a training college for the Sudan People's Liberation Movement (which now dominates the Government of South Sudan). There are still bunkers in the compound, built for protection against aerial bombardment.

By the time I arrived St Augustine's had been restored to its role as a school. But practically everything a school needs was lacking: it was chronically understaffed; there were insufficient desks and hardly any text books. I had to work out how to teach with just a blackboard and a map of the world. The situation was complicated by the fact that until recently secondary schools in the Equatorias had been following the Ugandan syllabus. After the independence of South Sudan most schools changed to the new, four-year South Sudan Certificate of Education. The students didn't like it, saying that no one would respect the new certificate. But the teachers, including the Ugandan teachers, insisted that now South Sudan was independent, they had to embrace the national syllabus.

I was given a room in the fathers' house, a guest house with five rooms. The house was shared, variously, with Brian Madison, one of the South Sudanese doctors from the hospital, Maggie Pacho, a Kenyan who was in charge of the malaria control program, and, later, Mama Magdalene, an agronomist, feminist and lay activist. In the village Maggie was nicknamed *Habboba* Malaria (Grandma Malaria) and I became *Habboba Khawaja* (Grandma Foreigner). In the school and in the fathers' compound we had electricity for a few hours a day, from 7 PM to 10 PM. Meals were cooked for the guests by the cook-housekeeper and we ate them when we wanted, often eating together, sometimes alone, depending on our schedules. The basic meal was beans and porridge made from maize or sorghum, with a sauce of greens, and sometimes dried fish or meat. When Maggie Malaria returned to Isohe after some months away she looked at me and said "this *khawaja* eats too little *posho* and is losing weight; you will have to cook her rice or she will fade away." And so they did.

Each day in Isohe began at 7.30, with an assembly: the students lined up in front of the teachers and duty prefects, uniforms were examined, then the students marched to the classrooms. The school and the church had their own rhythm: there were five days of teaching; then compulsory agriculture on Saturdays; and on Sunday morning mass at 10am, usually lasting until 12.30 or 1 PM at least. I took Stakhanovite pleasure in setting an example on Saturdays, wielding the hoe myself, much to the students' amusement.

In the years I taught there secondary teachers in South Sudan were paid appallingly low salaries, equivalent to US $100–200 a month. Salaries for primary teachers were even lower, equivalent to US $50–100 a month; they were often unable to pay the school fees for their own children. Nearly all the teachers had left their families behind in their home villages to come and work in Isohe. I received what I later found out to be the highest salary in the school: 1,250 South Sudan pounds (SSP), at that time equivalent to US $250 a month. It was as much as the head teacher's, but it took a year for me to be registered as a paid teacher with the Eastern Equatoria State Ministry of Education, so during that year the head would give me a handout of SSP 200 every two months or so, which covered a proportion of my expenses of SSP 200 (US $50) for a month's board and lodging at the fathers' house.

The head teacher of St Augustine's, Jackson Lopul, was a local man who had worked at every sort of job to push himself through school certificate in Khartoum and eventually get into University there. His energy was enormous – walking twelve kilometers to work on his farm and twenty kilometers to pick up teachers' salaries from the county education department in Ikotos. There was only one woman teacher apart from me. She was an excellent role model: tall and elegant, she taught commerce with great confidence. But she had had to leave her children behind in Uganda, the salary she was paid was not enough to live on, and one of her children had serious pancreatic problems; so she left around the same time as I did. This meant that the school, where nearly a third of the students were girls, was without a woman teacher for the following four years.

Both St Augustine's and the St Kizito Primary School were jointly run by the Ministry of Education and the Catholic Diocese of Torit (DOT); the state Ministry of Education paid the teachers' salaries and visited the schools from time to time to inspect them; while the diocese had oversight in more intangible ways. During my first year in Isohe nothing much happened, but during my second year the DOT assistant education officer, Richard Oyet, a former child soldier (he had been in Isohe when it was a training centre for the Sudan People's Liberation Army, and ended up in Australia), would come often, encouraging the school to be self-sustaining in agriculture, talking to the teachers and organizing training sessions.

Corporal punishment was routine. In one of Richard Oyet's training sessions he launched into a tirade against it and for a few weeks after I didn't see any beatings. But apart from this short period both boys and girls were beaten frequently. Boys would make it a matter of pride to leap up laughing after they had been caned. To me it was abhorrent to watch a girl lying sideways on the ground waiting to be beaten, often by a male teacher. But I was the only European in the school, and I decided that I would not criticise anything I saw or heard, unless a life was in danger. When corporal punishment took place, I left and walked away, so my colleagues could see I didn't like it, but I would say nothing.

There were two international NGOs working out of Isohe. One was an Italian organisation, AVSI, the Association of Volunteers in International Service, working in health care and, most importantly for us, in education, supporting the primary school and sponsoring some through secondary school. Few girls in the region would have gone to school without AVSI support. The other NGO was the Catholic organisation Caritas, working in agricultural projects. We had no internet at the Father's house, but there was access in the AVSI office and in the evening or at weekends, I would go there to read and write emails. I spent a lot of time preparing lessons, using what text books I could find; having a computer and internet access meant I was luckier than every other teacher. It was in the AVSI office that I wrote most of the letters home collected in this book.

One of the most important aspects of my life in Isohe was learning Dongotono. There were many variants of Lotuho I could have tried to learn, including Logir and Lotuho proper, but the mountains surrounding us were the Dongotono mountains, and the local people were Dongotono. The Comboni missionaries who built up Isohe in the decades after it was established in 1924 would certainly have learnt their language; people told me that a Mexican priest had learnt it in 1990s. There are about 20,000 speakers of Dongotono. It seems that the higher you go in the mountains the purer or more antique the form of the language they speak.

I am not good at languages myself, though I speak some Sudanese Arabic, but I enjoy them, so I determined that I would learn Dongotono. One evening during my first term In Isohe, walking in the pitch dark on the rutted roadway back from AVSI, the Italian NGO, I met a group of women and girls, almost invisible in the darkness. One of them returned my greeting in impeccable English. "What is your name?" I asked. "Elizabeth," came the reply. "But mine is also Elizabeth!" I said. Learning that she was a Dongotono speaker, I implored her to come and visit me in the Parish and consider giving me lessons. Elizabeth Kuti turned out to be a former St Augustine's student and she taught me for a very happy six months thereafter. She got a short-term job with AVSI, but later left, rather unwillingly, to get married. Then I took lessons with Ohide Johnson. He would still be my Dongotono teacher today, supposing that I was still learning Dongotono, which, alas, I am not.

After two years teaching in the school I left South Sudan in December 2013. It was just before the massacres of Nuer on the streets of Juba and the resultant civil war between the follow-ers of the president, Salva Kiir, and the former vice-president,

Riek Machar. In the years that followed this conflict triggered mass death, rape, destruction and the forcible displacement of millions of South Sudanese. By contrast the period that I spent in Isohe seems like a time of peace – but of course it was not. There was already widespread fighting in the country – with a leader of the Murle people, David Yau Yau, in conflict with the government in neighbouring Jonglei State, and growing cattle raids and fighting between villages in areas of Eastern Equatoria. The threat of greater conflict was constant; in the teaching of church leaders peace and reconciliation was a constant theme.

The area round Isohe is almost entirely Catholic, and, with no non-Catholics in the area, there is no great impetus for ecumenical feeling (though in Ikotos, twenty kilometers away, the African Inland Mission, which is a protestant missionary organisation, maintains a school). The Parish priest was the most important figure for us, more important than the local chief (who didn't usually come to church) or the local state government administrator (who did). When I arrived the incumbent priest was Father Taban, but he left after some months to pursue further studies in Kampala. Father Anthony, who had previously been the parish priest, returned after completing his master's degree in Education, having written a dissertation on problems hindering education of girls in South Sudan. He was succeeded by Father Ben, who is still the parish priest today.

Different priests have different styles; Father Anthony was much loved by the teachers and by the staff of the NGOs and the hospital in Isohe, holding open discussions in the compound where a circle of up to a dozen would sit round debating the affairs of the world. Father Ben, on the other hand, who was born in the area, was more grounded in the parish, visiting all the outlying churches – often just mud-brick buildings or spaces under trees – and the catechists in the different villages, calling them in for consultations, organising parish council meetings, and encouraging youth to play football. Father Ben was – and is – also very energetic in enabling the women of the area to play an active part in all aspects of life: in literacy classes, discussion groups, agricultural development, and in communal reconciliation. Under his aegis, life in Isohe widened considerably while I was there, and has continued to do so since.

Acknowledgments

Thanks to my friends in South Sudan who treated their elderly *khawaja* colleague with such lovingkindness. First and foremost among them is the late Sister Rose Adiero, my initial contact and later dear friend, who sent me to Isohe, and subsequently founded her own school, the Sacred Heart School at Aliyya, near Palotaka. Sister Rose suffered an untimely death in 2017. Like so many deaths in South Sudan it was the result of a road accident, while she was travelling on the back of a motorcycle from the Sacred Heart School to the nearby town of Magwi. Other sisters of the Sacred Heart order in Isohe also became close friends and advisers, most of all Sister Paskwina Iromo (in these letters sometimes referred to as Sister P.) who founded the St Kizito primary school in Isohe, and was its headmistress for nineteen years; also Sisters Helen, Theresa, Theresina and Felicita, and others in Isohe and Juba.

I benefited from the support and company of the priests who worked in Isohe or visited us there, and others I met in Torit or Juba. Foremost among them is Father Ben – Father Peter Ben Louis – still fighting ceaselessly for peace and progress in his parish today. Then there was Father James Taban Clement, who was the first priest to welcome me to Isohe, Father Anthony Ubeo, who became a close friend and adviser, and Father Kalisto

Lokuya, with whom I had so many long and interesting discussions. Other sources of inspiration were the late Father John Baptist Lohitu, a wise and joyful priest who retired to Isohe, and – in Torit – Father Okello, the late Bishop Johnson Akio Mutek, bishop of Torit, and Bishop Paride Taban, bishop emeritus of Torit.

Among the staff of St Augustine's I should mention four names above all: Jackson Lopul, the head teacher, Stephen Opito, Arkanjelo Lomuno, and John Batiste – all local people. Three of them arrived to teach after I left, but I met them earlier when they came on teaching practice. It is they who have been responsible for turning the school around in the last few years, overcoming the difficulties chronicled in these letters, and making it the success that it is today, My thanks also to those who welcomed me when I first arrived in Isohe – to mention only a few, Lokulang Faustino, Tartisio Abuna, and Orisa Ambrose – and the succession of good teachers from Uganda, both those who left and those who stayed: Lorisa (Lucy) Layet, Emmanuel Obita, Geoffrey Odokonyero, and James Akena.

I am grateful for the companionship of those who, like me, were guests of the Parish in Isohe: Maggie Pacho, the organizer of the malaria programme; Mama Magdalene (Magdalene Atiol Biato – Mama M. in some of these letters); Dr Brian Madison, Arsenal supporter and unbeatable Scrabble player; Charles Anteros, former child soldier and companion on several research missions; and Charles Ogachi, diocesan engineer for a period, and builder of the women's centre In Isohe. It was Charles who saved my life when I had malaria – by remarking on my absence from breakfast.

Also to those working for international NGOs in Isohe: Gabriele Erba, climber of mountains, Maria Gaudenzi, Andrea, Onen

David Livingstone, Mairi Eliphas and many other friends from AVSI; Lokunyang Justin from Caritas; and John Dario Ohide, formerly of AVSI and Caritas, Chair of the Board of Governors of St Augustine's School. Above all, I am grateful to my two dear Dongotono teachers, Elizabeth Kuti, whose wonderful stories from her grandmother I will publish some day, and Ohide Johnson Paul, who became my principal research collaborator, teaching me not just the language, but much of what I know about his home area.

Thanks also to my *khawaja* friends: to Eddie Thomas, who introduced me to Sister Rose and has been a rock of support throughout, and to John Ryle, who gave me helpful advice before I left, and thought my letters home worth publishing – first on the Rift Valley Institute website, then with some revisions, in this book. In South Sudan, Eddie Thomas, John Ryle, Joanna Oyediran and Diana Felix da Costa all made the difficult journey to visit me in Isohe. Thanks also to those I travelled with elsewhere in South Sudan, while working for Amnesty International: Khairun Dhala and Nyagoah Tut, admirable researchers and good companions. For editorial advice and assistance, many thanks to John Dario Ohide, John Raymond, Ohide Johnson Paul and Joanna Oyediran, and, for the use of their photographs of Isohe, to Fabricio Marra, Javier Sauras, John Ryle, Brett Morton and AVSI.

Finally there are the students of St Augustine whom I taught and who taught me. They remained attentive to this *khawaja habboba* with an accent so hard to understand. I hope they will all have the success and joy in life which they deserve.

Father Kalisto, Sister Paskwina, Father Ben, Mama Magdalene, Sister Theresa and Elizabeth Hodgkin, St Theresa's Church compound.

FIRST LETTER

How do you study when there's nothing to eat?

July 2012... Start of term in an empty school... A human rights class... But no textbooks... No mobile network... No transport... And no fruit... Life in the hunger gap... Cultivation days... A ban on cards and dominoes.

A new term is starting in Isohe, where I've come to teach in the secondary school, St Augustine's. Isohe (sometimes spelt Isoke, and rhyming, more or less, with "it's okay") is an isolated, beautiful valley, surrounded by mountains, with no public transport or mobile telephone network and infrequent internet access. The mango season is over now and there is no fruit in the market; only local greens or beans on sale. It's the first of July.

So far the teaching staff comprises only the head teacher and myself. Pupils trickle in – about 25 by the end of the first week – but many from around Isohe do not bother. At the school there is a general feeling that nothing much is going to happen yet, with pupils doing little but cleaning, sweeping or cutting the grass. Better to have them at home working on the land. Last term there were no students for two weeks. But there are a few more this term and the head and I are both more active.

I am teaching a human rights class, human rights being included, optimistically, among the subjects in the new South Sudan national syllabus. The class benefits from the presence of seven Nuba students, refugees from fighting up north in Sudan, who are able to describe how the Nuba cannot get jobs in offices there. They explain to the rest of the class the meaning of the word "discrimination". These Nuba students were evacuated with their whole school from South Kordofan, a place that is currently the scene of violent clashes between the Sudanese army and a [?] movement with links to South Sudan. The students have been distributed among schools here in Eastern Equatoria.

There are still almost no textbooks. Up to now, for the history class, I have been writing my own version of the history of Europe in longhand and giving it out on pages torn from an exercise book. Soon, though, we will be able to use second-hand textbooks donated by a school in Durham. Carrying them out here, my luggage was fifteen kilos overweight, but the Kenya Airways check-in desk at Nairobi airport waved me through.

This is an oral society, though. I am reminded of it all the time. I set an essay for one class: should more funds be given to agriculture than to education? They said it was too difficult for them. But when it came to the class debate they discussed the question vigorously. Likewise, they stay silent during my lectures on the French Revolution (vivid though they are). The class members said they were understanding me "a hundred per cent", but they wouldn't ask any questions at all. Then, during the Friday afternoon school debate under the mahogany tree, one of them spoke passionately about liberty, equality and fraternity.

How narrow their lives are, though. There are no newspapers and no radio. They sometimes seem hardly to know that the rest of the world exists. Maybe some can understand *liberté, egalité* and *fraternité*, but they don't know where France is. Debating and football are the only recreations.

In January this year, South Sudan shut down oil production in a dispute with Sudan – the country from which it broke away a year ago – over the charges levied by the North for using the pipeline to the Red Sea. Since the closure of the oil pipeline, the rise in food prices has become a major issue. Maize, the main staple, rose from sixty South Sudan pounds for a fifty-kilo sack in 2011 (around US $20 or £12 sterling) to 150 South Sudan pounds in April this year (£30 or US $50), then to SSP 250 (US $85 or £55 sterling) as term was starting at the end of May. Last term in Isohe both the primary school – St Kizito's – and the secondary school closed a week early, having run out of food. Our school fees, at SSP 250 a term for full board, would have covered the food, but too many fees were unpaid, and a number of students dropped out in March. Parents in urban schools are more likely to find money, in rural areas agriculture is almost entirely for household consumption. The head teacher rails against fathers: "They'll find cows for another wife but not to send their children to school." This term eighteen students couldn't pay the fees. And another ten look as though they may not be able to. My Senior Three class is halved. One of my students says his parents have cattle, but only for his bridewealth. They want him to get a wife.

These are the hunger months before harvest. The World Food Programme distributes food but nothing has yet arrived. Before the school closed towards the end of last term, pupils sometimes had only one meal a day. The first two weeks of this term there was torrential rain each day; a World Food Programme lorry taking maize to primary schools in Torit, 180 kilometers from here, got stuck in the road and was plundered by men with pangas. They cut open the 100 kg sacks to make them lighter to carry.

Local people say the whole thing was a set-up. "A child could see the vehicle was unsuitable for these roads," said a worker from the diocese of Torit. In another incident, after drinking heavily, three villagers near Lobira ambushed a lorry carrying sacks of maize, killing a passenger.

With food prices so high, everyone is taking cultivation much more seriously. When two more teachers arrived after the start of term, the head teacher disappeared to work on his own land. State governments have declared Fridays national agriculture days. Those living in our compound – South Sudanese and Ugandans mostly working for the hospital or NGOs – joke about how public servants in Juba, the capital, will be watering their throats with beer or *kwete* – the local homebrew – and planting playing cards. The same assessment may have led the government to announce punishments for those who play card games – or dominoes or Ludo – on cultivation days.

Teachers' salaries are low in any case, and they are paid in South Sudanese pounds, so they have seen their salaries cut in half. The maths teacher has still not arrived, three weeks after the beginning of term. Last term he said to me: "I am wondering if it is worth continuing if I cannot support my family." For six months we have had no chemistry teacher: now two doctors and some nurses and technical staff have agreed to split classes between them. The science, maths and commerce teachers are all Ugandans; if they leave the school will collapse.

Schoolchildren on the steps of St Theresa's Church.

SECOND LETTER

Who will be the next parish priest?

October 2012... The origins of the Isohe mission... The valley where buffalo roamed... The year of faith... The other St Teresa... Cabbages... Cassava... A five-hour mass... A true crime exclusive... the new chemistry teacher.

The parish priest has left to pursue a master's degree in Kampala in public administration. To be parish priest of Isohe is a big responsibility. And since he left we have suffered from his absence.

Isohe was founded by the Comboni Fathers in the 1920s, in this beautiful fertile valley under the mountains. Before they came, buffalo roamed here. (It's true. I've verified it in interviews and archival research). *La bella Isohe* was what the Combonis called this place. It became a parish in 1926. The parish priest was effectively the ruler of the area and the village of Isohe grew up round the mission. Nearly everything here is under the authority of the Diocese of Torit: the secondary school with a hundred pupils, the primary school with over a thousand, the hospital, and the Centre for Food Security across the river, run by the Catholic charity Caritas. Only AVSI, an Italian non-governmental organization that works in health and education – has some independence.

So the question is: who will be the next parish priest? It's like a Trollope novel. I have just downloaded *The Warden* onto my Kindle. Our head teacher is currently in charge of the parish, by election in his role as as parish pastoral chairperson. The acting priest is Father Ben, a Dongotono from this area. Father Ben is also the bishop's secretary, so he is a powerful person and committed to rebuilding the glories of Isohe. He drives himself over from Torit on Saturday evenings to take Mass and returns on Sunday evening. We were told that the Year of Faith would be launched last Thursday from Isohe, but in the end the bishop couldn't come, nor could Father Ben, as he had malaria. And the internet was down so I couldn't find out what exactly the Year of Faith was.

Isohe, I learn, was first visited by the Comboni Fathers on St Teresa's Day, which is 1 October. So St Teresa – without an h – is our patron saint. And we were to have a big celebration for that day – only a week late. I was sorry to discover, though, that this St Teresa is not the interesting mystic St Teresa of Ávila, but St Teresa dell Bambino Gesu, a sickly nineteenth-century Italian who used the elevator as a symbol to illustrate her assertion that even the weak, who couldn't climb the steps, could get to the Kingdom of Heaven. Father Ben revealed this to us this in a speech after the Mass. But who here knows what an elevator is? It is hardly an appropriate image, in any case, for these mountains where elderly women of my age walk four hours down to the valley in a morning carrying cabbages or onions and four hours up again in the evening carrying cassava roots on their heads.

There were 126 children to be baptised and I guessed the Mass would last at least three hours. In fact it lasted nearly five; after that the Ugandan teachers left in disgust. They missed the bull cooked for lunch – and the choirs. The school drama group put on a play, in a mixture of English, Lotuho, and Juba Arabic: it was about a sick girl and her drunken, non-church-going father and brothers. The boys were excellent at playing the parts of drunken yobs. The bad father and his sons take the girl to the diviner (brilliantly acted), who demanded a goat (bleating a lot) and several hundred pounds, and made cuts in her flesh supposedly to cure her. When she was finally taken to hospital it was too late to save her. The play featured a nun and a priest who crossed himself furiously all the time, to much laughter. It showed that the students are better at creating what they want to do (they only spent a day rehearsing it) than doing what others want.

For example, the school newspaper. I tried to organise this and it took two weeks to get on to the wall, though at least at that point everyone was pleased with it. The headlines were not exactly compelling: "Uprooting Groundnuts was Started Two Weeks Ago in Isohe Boma" was one of the highlights. Many articles, like the one in question, went on to say: "And now the news in detail". But it is true that, for the last two weeks, everybody has been uprooting groundnuts and putting them out to dry. That is the story here. The author also recorded the cost of things in the market. These included the shocking price hike in 96-page exercise books from SSP 2 to SSP 4 (from US 50 cents to US $1, or 30p to 60p in UK currency). Students have to buy their own exercise books and the lack of them is becoming a problem.

We got an exclusive story that day as there was gunfire quite close. Ohisa, who comes from Isohe and seems to know what is happening, wrote an article then and there with the basic details. A local Dongotono man was wounded in the head with a panga by some Logir who were carrying supplies of *liralira*. (*Liralira* is Ugandan style distilled alcohol; the Logir people are neighbours of the Dongotono.) The cause of the fight is obscure; it seems the assailants wanted to beat up someone who wasn't there at the time; the actual victim was their second choice. It shows that Isohe is not quite the haven of peace I once believed.

In theory a killer may take refuge in the parish (i.e. our compound) where the victim's family won't kill him, but will allow him be handed over to the police. I'm not sure whether that will work, though. It seems I am the senior person in the compound now. On Saturday I had to break up a fight when a drunken teacher slapped the assistant cleaner on her cheek and she pursued him with an iron bar.

Our new chemistry teacher, W., is really good value. This term he arrived first of all the teachers (except for the head). He walked the last twenty miles from Ikotos. Last term when he applied I was saying cautiously to the head, "You must take up his references". I could not imagine why someone like him with a diploma in science education from a British university would want to come to Isohe, where he might be paid at most US $400 a month (but would more likely not receive a cent till after March when oil money may flow again). But taking up references is not a South Sudan thing, certainly where there is no e-mail, and W., like most people in Africa, carried all his twenty or more certificates with him – all his degrees and diplomas, including one certifying his skills in growing vegetables for the UK market. Meanwhile I arrived here empty handed, with no academic certificates at all.

W. is always cheerful; and walking with him is a joy. He notices everything. The golden flecks in the Iwali River might actually be gold, he says, so he'll have the students panning. And, he says, he will get them to gather the iron-rich deposits and show them simple smelting techniques. During classes this afternoon I saw him coming back from somewhere with the senior students clustered all around him. He told me that he had decided in 2005, following the Comprehensive Peace Agreement, that he ought to teach in South Sudan. Then, in Leeds, he googled the phrase "South Sudan teaching chemistry" and found the post here advertised. So he came to Isohe knowing little more than the name, like me, without even the links I had to the diocese and the sisters.

Mama Magdalene, on the road to Lolit

The feast of Christ the King

November 2012... A crate of Coca-cola... A sermon on
gender-based violence... Empowerment and evangelization...
The Isohe women's movement...School fees, girls, cows and
kwete... Do I have immunity to malaria?

The parish compound consists of our five-bedroomed guest-house surrounded by the huts of others living in the compound: three orphans, three staff and occasional guests. This Saturday we woke to find the compound full of goods brought from Torit by the indefatigable Father Ben. He arrived at one o'clock last night. The haul includes fifteen crates of Coca-cola and Fanta, mango juice, sugar and sorghum.

It puts me in mind of Ho Chi Minh's complaint: whenever a Vietnamese village could find an excuse, he used to say, they would kill a pig and throw a party. Here in Isohe, on Saturday night, they killed a bull. Before that there was St Teresa's feast day (our patron saint); then the launch of the Year of Faith (when neither the promised Bishop nor the bull materialised), and All Saints' Day, and – just this Sunday – the feast of Christ the King. The Feast of Christ the King ushers in sixteen days of women's activism and peace-building. It is marked by Ugandan disco music, dancing and cooking. This goes on outside the parish offices in front of the Church till 4 AM.

Then there was a procession followed by a three-hour Mass in an impressively packed church: about 800 people including beaded dancers from Woroworo and Chahari and small children packed into every pew. Father Ben's sermon about the kingdom of heaven ranged from the Book of Daniel to Revelation. Towards the end he informed the congregation in a furious tone "If you are in a house with gender-based violence and violence against women, that is not the kingdom of heaven". Immediately there was clapping and ululation. It was surprising to me that the congregation – mostly women – could understand the meaning of the English phrase "gender-based violence" without waiting for the translation. Also that they were still listening to a sermon after forty minutes. They will definitely inherit the earth.

We still don't have a parish priest and I wonder if we ever will. Father Ben, the bishop's secretary, is deeply committed to Isohe. He is aiming to take this isolated valley – without public transport or a mobile phone network – back to the position it enjoyed under the Comboni Fathers from the 1920s to the 1950s, when Isohe was the dominant church centre for the eastern part of Eastern Equatoria, an area about half the size of England. So the church has embraced a combination of agricultural development, women's empowerment and evangelisation. One plan is to develop a large area of fertile land at Lolit Bridge, away to the north-west, to solve food problems for the schools and provide sorghum for the whole area. (At present, apart from what is locally sold in small piles in the market, all the sacks of sorghum are from Uganda.)

An Italian group called Solidale Italia came for a week to get women to raise their self-esteem. They stayed with the sisters but upset them, saying that education – which is the main aim in Sister Paskwina's life – could be bad, leading people away from their culture towards television. Television is something the sisters deeply love. They often watch TV, especially Mexican soaps, in the evening. The Italian group were only here for week anyway.

The Isohe women's movement is genuinely local. One of the activists is called Mama Magdalene. She is from Chukudum and was formerly a state minister. She is said to have resigned because of corruption. She's here a few days a fortnight and spends her whole time talking to the women. They plan to plant an orchard behind the school where now there are huts. She says the owners won't mind moving as they know they have encroached on Church land. And all the land here belongs to the Church, through the cleverness of the Combonis back in 1927. A simple women's centre is being built in local brick – it's been going up fast between the Church and the school, overseen by Charles, the efficient, modest Kenyan diocesan engineer.

Some students here have their fees paid by sponsors who have entrusted me with the responsibility for selecting and administering the funds. I spoke to all nineteen of the spon-sored students about their families two weeks ago. In the end I thought that perhaps three of them could have found the money themselves. Two of them were top in their class and wrote me long letters about their problems, but one of them (whose mother used to make *kwete* alcohol to pay his school fees) is living with a cousin by marriage who works at the hospital and who is sending his own son to a private school in Uganda (about US $250 a term) and the other has a brother in Torit with two wives. Then there was N. from Chahari, behind the mountain. I asked about his family. His parents were poor, he said, and he had one sister aged twenty.

"Did she go to school?" I asked.

"No, she never went to school, she got married last year".

"Then you are rich, you have 21 cows," I said.

"No, they only paid us ten".

"Even one cow would cover school fees for four terms," I said.

"No," he said, "They all died."

"You expect me to believe that?" I asked him.

"Half of them died and half of them were raided."

"And now you expect me to believe that too?" I said.

We only have two girls on the list, one is in her last term and used to make *kwete* for her school fees. When R. told me her sister had just got married I left it at that; she was on the head-teacher's first list of poor students. Later I told the head about the conversation with N.

"Yes," he said, "A lot of cows are dying now. It's that disease you have in England. Mad cow?"

"Mad cow disease?" I said "Then we'll all die!"

"No, not the brain, just the lungs".

"Is it TB?"

"Yes – but the meat is perfectly all right as long as it's cooked. They are dying because they've run out of vaccine".

The only cows pastoralists will sell off are sick ones. So none of what the head said fills me with confidence about our meat. Many people I know here have had brucellosis. On the second day the meat is smoked and smells and I now don't eat it. The same day Livingstone, water engineer in the compound, said he had malaria but the hospital was running out of anti-malaria drugs. I have stopped taking prophylaxis myself since I ran out at the end of September. I have been lucky not to catch anything. A lot of the teachers have been going down with malaria. There are more mosquitoes in the gardens behind the school than in the well-swept parish compound. Hopefully I have some immunity. When I travelled with my father Thomas in Ethiopia, sharing his room in the cheapest hotel he could find (usually a brothel with plywood walls) he would be slapping himself all night, yet I would be OK.

I will leave the attempts to get Julius Nyerere declared a saint to the next letter. [For the young, Nyerere was the first President of Tanzania]. As usual we have run out of food, so exams start on Monday.

Sister Paskwina

FOURTH LETTER

The violent months

December 2012... No food, so term is ended... A kidnapped
bride... The difference between women and men... Praying
to St Julius Nyerere... I do not have immunity to malaria
after all... Trying to read *On The Road*.

I t's December and term ended early again – and once again
because of food. This time I don't think it's incompetence,
though it is true that neither the head, nor the deputy head
nor the director of studies have any management training and
don't do things like attendance registers. I don't think they even
recorded the exam marks of the pupils since we put them on to
single report cards which were given to the students. The truth
is that the school is not economically viable with less than 120
pupils, and it now has only 91.

Last Friday evening , a week ago, I was sitting under the
stars chatting with Charles, the Kenyan engineer, when we
heard gunshots, followed by ululations. We were relieved
at the ululations, suggesting that it was a marriage and
not a fight. But if we had been more aware we should have
realised that the gunshots meant that it was a marriage by
kidnapping: the girl carried away was R., the one girl left
among our sponsored students. In general, when a girl is

carried away it is because she has agreed to it; a goat is left in the compound instead of the girl who is returned after five days; the man is symbolically beaten, and then pays the bride price. But my teacher, Elizabeth Kuti, told me of one of her friends who was abducted unwillingly, and is now living unhappily in a village behind the mountains with two children.

The head teacher was furious. R.'s father told him: "Well of course if she had shouted we would have roused all the neighbours, but if a girl is carried away and does not even cry out, what are we to think? That she is accepting it."

Sister Paskwina was bitterly upset. "One by one," she said, "all the girls in her class have left to be married, in Primary Five, Primary Six and Primary Seven. She was the last of our hopes".

I have been shy of calling each girl to ask them about their situation for fear that it would encourage hard luck stories, but I think R.'s case gives the chance to do it as a protection, not a financial measure. She had been poor in her school work in the first term, but once she got the sponsorship she had moved into boarding and did well. I sent a message to her saying that education need never be ended whether you are married or not, and she should try to continue; her new husband is a trader down in the village, and if he can pay the 25 cows then he can afford to pay school fees.

On the day after the end of term – brought forward because of the food shortage – Mama M., the Catholic evangelist feminist agriculturalist ex-State Minister, gave a workshop to the seniors of the Secondary School on women's empowerment and peace-building. That was after Father Ben had given the initial session on the family.

The story starts, of course with Adam and Eve, showing that humans are meant to be part of a family. (One student said

"What about priests?") Reproductive differences come from God. Mama Magdalene spoke about gender and was wonderful at acting women behaving as men and men behaving as women, mincing along on the ground under the mango trees in her high-heeled shoes, avoiding a projecting rock that I would have tripped over a dozen times. She is clearly fascinated by sex-change operations and called on me to speak about them the second day. This was my only intervention till I was called to speak at the end.

Apart from unchangeable God-given reproductive differences, we learned that there is no difference whatsoever between men and women. Women can do anything a man can do (and Mama M. clearly felt they should be able to become priests as well.) There is a plan for a large increase in the number of women catechists and the empowerment of women by giving them plots of land in the new Lolit Bridge enterprise. This, it was explained, will keep families together and diminish violence. Then we moved into peace-building, starting in the family and moving outwards.

But there has been more violence. Education does not stop this. A former seminarian, while drunk, beat his wife. When I left Isohe she was still in a coma, her husband holding vigil beside her bed, swearing he'd kill the doctors and then himself if they didn't save her.

November and December are generally violent months. Perhaps it is because there is less agricultural work to do. There is less money about and attacking trucks carrying goods on the road becomes tempting. A truck was shot at on the road from Uganda and the Senior Threes, doing school certificate next year, are worried that the Ugandan teachers will leave. There is local violence between the Logir and Dongotono but the basis seems to be personal – alcohol and cattle-related rather than due to tribal animosity. The head teacher gave a long lecture to the students against tribalism – he said it had been reported that some students were giving bigger helpings of food to people of their area. Next day, sitting under the staff room tree, he gave me a lecture on what he claimed was the particularly violent history of the Logir. Unlike the Dongotono, he said, the Logir people like stealing and killing. A child of a mixed marriage can kill his uncle, so it's bad to marry with a Logir. In Chorokol, he said, they don't go to school because even small children spend their time practicing raiding cattle.

Yet Sister Paskwina, who revived the primary school in Isohe, is a Logir. After the incident last week, the Logir were (she says, falsely) accused of plundering a truck carrying property of the member of parliament for Lobira. So the police (but are they really police?) were sent to her village of Hiriafit, where they plundered her and her brother's houses, taking mattresses, clothes, plates and cups. The Honourable, she said, referring to the MP, was just taking revenge, since obviously neither she nor her brother had anything to do with it. "The Honourable" – with the H pronounced – is a term that is often used to talk of MPs, Ministers, their large houses and ostentatious wealth, usually with venom.

As term was ending, amid the crisis of printing exam papers I went to collect the printer to take it to the primary school. Geoffrey, the agriculture teacher, called a tough-looking boy to carry it. Then he lifted it himself. "Ah no!" he said. "This is too heavy. It needs a lady." So a smallish Senior One girl put it on her head and carried it down to the Primary School. In this culture men can't carry things on their heads. On the way the Senior One girl told me how hungry they were these days.

Father A. was here for most of October, but instead of becoming priest in charge in Isohe he has now chosen to accept an offer to go to Cedar Falls to minister to the Americans. When he was here he told me that everyone was praying to the late Julius Nyerere, the first President of Tanzania, hoping he would perform miracles and become a saint. You don't have to do much in the way of miracles to be a saint, it seems. According to Father A., a Jesuit priest prayed to St Teresa dell Bambino Gesu, Isohe's patron saint, to send him a red rose and then to send a white rose, which she did, by the hand of passers-by.

In childhood my own prayers were always extremely personal and selfish. Accordingly, while I was in Juba I asked Julius Nyerere to ensure that I would be given money when I went to the bank and that I should not be mugged. And everything went like clockwork. Sister V. gave me a lift to the bank in the Sisters' land cruiser. You feel secure with a Sister beside you. The miracle was that, after more than a month, money that I had ordered by a Skype call had actually arrived in South Sudan, a country the teller in the Cooperative Bank in Britain had never heard of. So now I think that Nyerere should definitely be canonised.

Finally, just a week after I made hubristic remarks about my resistance to malaria – at the beginning of the dry season, when there are hardly any mosquitoes about – I caught malaria. Robert Somali, the clinician at Isohe hospital administered the test and advised me to that I would be sick for some days. "Take book!" he said. And I thought, what wise advice. So I took *On the Road*, an uncut 1963 Pan edition from a Dutch library, one of those books I should have read at the age of seventeen and was now reading at 71.

What he meant, though, was not that I should take a book to entertain myself, but that I had forgotten to pick up the school exercise book that held the record of my case. This is the only thing we have to pay for at Isohe Hospital. It says "Elizabeth PRUDENCE – 70" on the front, and the diagnosis "uncomp malaria" inside. I still don't know so much about having malaria, uncomp or not, but the cure – Amodiaquine – was horrible. It only takes three days, but for two days you just lie there, retching, with cramps, and of course unable to read, even Jack Kerouac.

In the fathers' compound, St Theresa's parish church

FIFTH LETTER

Everything is bearable if you have bread

March 2013... The Ugandan teachers have not arrived... Crossing the Iwali river... The problem of salaries... Dust storms... Dongotono etymology... The women's centre is lacking a ceiling... Life in an ecclesiocracy.

It's March; term is already into its fourth week and still the Ugandan teachers have not arrived. But the mobile network, which you can find by walking three kilometers, finally started working again. And last Sunday afternoon the head teacher and I and two others walked the three kilometers to be connected. No need now to take off our shoes to wade across the Iwali River. It can be jumped over or crossed with stepping stones. Below the mountains, huts were perched on rocks half way up; there were bells from goats wandering on the summits, and a dance on a dancing ground near the road. People passed us dressed up for it: one jubilant woman had made a headdress with bands and upright pages from an old exercise book.

"She is showing her pride because her daughter is going to school", said the head teacher. The primary school mentor, from the Madi people in the West of Eastern Equatoria State, commented on the fertility of the land. "The Madi would leave none of this uncultivated!" he said. "You could grow vegetables by the river all the year round, and rice and sugar cane..." Depressed, the head teacher agreed. In 2001, he said, Father Mawa had made a vegetable garden by the river, but now there is nothing.

I myself came two weeks late for the beginning of term, as I had been accompanying the new Amnesty International South Sudan researcher on a visit to Wau. I expected to be one week late, but we were delayed by flight problems. I am a conscientious teacher, so I felt embarrassed, but even so I was back before some of the others. That week and this there have been only the South Sudanese teachers and me. At first we would teach without a timetable, bargaining as we left the staffroom. "Oh, are you going to Senior Four now? Then I'll go to Senior Three..." Then we agreed on a timetable, which we don't always keep to, and the students haven't bothered to copy, just waiting to see what lesson turns up. So I've been getting students who have dropped history attending history lessons. "Oh, let's stay," they say, "we are not doing anything else".

Also the primary school leaving results were late, so Senior One has only just started registering. Numbers so far are not yet up to last year, but students are still arriving. As for the Ugandan teachers, when we reached them by phone from the three kilometer point, they said it was a question of money. They hadn't been paid and hadn't the money for bus fares, let alone leaving food for their families. Then two days ago two of them, including Obita, the Accounts teacher, arrived. But Obita immediately returned to Uganda, carrying two other salaries in cash for the stranded teachers.

There is no bank here in Isohe, nor in Ikotos, but there are branches of East African banks in Torit, and, of course, in Juba. Salaries could easily be paid so that Ugandan and Kenyan teachers could get them from their nearest town. But the Ministry of Education in Juba sends cash to the State Ministry of Education in Torit which sends cash to the education office for Ikwoto county in Ikotos, and the head teacher or senior staff member of each school throughout the rural areas comes to the county headquarters to collect the cash. Sometimes it hasn't yet arrived so they go back again. Many schools, like us, are not on a phone network and I don't think even the county HQ has email, so there may be no other way of knowing if the salaries have arrived. Ambrose, my fellow teacher, who is a former child soldier, says, cynically, that they pay in cash because it is easier to detach money at each stage.

This payment of salaries has allowed me to see that teachers are getting even lower salaries than I thought. James, our gentle Maths teacher who draws triangles for his students in the sand under the tree and gives them extra coaching on Saturdays, is paid less than US $100 a month. I am ashamed. I am now on the Ministry of Education books and get paid probably more than anyone. I am a Grade VII and get 1,013 South Sudan pounds a month, which is currently US $340 or UK £220 sterling. It feels like a vast amount. Yet one pound is the smallest unit of currency. Imagine – a country as poor as this, with the smallest unit of money worth twenty pence or thirty cents. How do people survive without small change?

This has been a time of dust storms. They are not as bad as the *habubs* of Khartoum, but quite strong, lots of dust blowing, and extreme heat. Wrinkles have suddenly appeared on my face like a river with many tributaries. As soon as I put sun-cream on, I want to put more. Small boys fly kites made of torn up plastic bags, with many fluttering plastic tails and knotted plastic cord. We are approaching the mango season and the trees are full of children picking and eating the unripe mangoes. I had my first slices of the hard, sweet mango windfalls given me by the Sisters today.

When I walked with a former student to Woroworo, half a dozen kilometers away, it was cloudy and cool. A lovely walk beside the mountains, with the Dongotono villages perched on ridges fifty meters above the plain. I learned that there are two etymologies proposed for the word "Dongotono". One is "people of the mountain". The other is "eating and mourning." This, it is said, is because they were people who did not know when they would get another meal. I favour the former derivation. At this season, after harvest, before the rains and the planting season, granaries and vats in store huts are piled high with sorghum; it is the other side of the mountain which has been suffering from a bad season.

Meanwhile I am observing, without being directly involved, the progress of two projects. Firstly, the Women's Centre. The diocesan building manager, Charles the Kenyan, is a genius. He was recruited on the spot by the Bishop of Torit who met him in Mumbai Airport on one of his medical visits to India. Charles builds very simply and cheaply, purely with local labour and locally-made bricks.

The weekend before last the head of UN Women in Sudan, a pugnacious Nigerian lady, came on a visit. I was afraid that she would think the building was so good that she would kidnap Charles. But not at all, she clearly felt the whole thing was a mistake. Isohe was not big enough to merit something like that. Why not build it in Kapoeta, further east? It is easy to see where she is coming from because there is a state-of-the-art Norwegian Hospital built in Katiko, in the east. And Katiko is the home village, apparently, of the State Minister of Health. But most of the sick still go to the Mission Hospital in Kapoeta twelve miles away. There must have seemed to her no good reason other than this sort of thing for siting a woman's centre in our remote village where there is nothing but farmers, schools, and an empty market. But the women here want it and a lot of them turn up for meetings, which always end in eating and drinking and dancing, and being smeared with flour. So let us see. At the moment Charles' local workers have built so quickly that the money has run out – and the workers, who are owed three weeks' salary, have gone on strike. I suppose UN Women will continue to fund the building. It now has a roof, windows, doors and lacks only a ceiling and a veranda.

The other project I am watching is the Lolit Bridge agricultural project. This is also a result of the energy of Father Ben, the bishop's secretary, and Mama Magdalene, in her role as food security officer of Caritas Torit. The parish has a vast tract of land at Lolit Bridge. The main idea is that it should grow sorghum so that there won't any longer be a need for importing it. They will distribute plots particularly to women (who don't inherit by custom). And the primary and secondary schools will become self-sufficient in food so we don't have to close when it runs out. It will be interesting to see if it works. The broken-down tractor in our compound is still not working. A large elderly tractor given a few years ago by the Italians was driven here under its own steam from Narus, some 150 kilometers away. But the ploughshares were taken somewhere else, so we are waiting for these. Walking fifteen kilometers to cultivate is a long distance for anyone to walk and then farm; one would need huts, food, water, cooking, a store, and supervision. Last year the school only cultivated five of the eleven acres of land that belong to it. But we had a good sorghum crop, which we've been eating, and by April we will have cassava too.

In this ecclesiocracy, the lack of a resident priest means the compound where I stay has become chaotic. We are four fairly permanent, easy-going, paying guests: Livingstone, a Ugandan water engineer, Charles, a Kenyan master builder, and Brian, a South Sudanese doctor. But the management has changed, and our housekeeper, who worked for the diocese for six years (for US $50 a month), has left and returned to her home in Magwi. So we have a succession of local people to cook. They are all very nice, but always seem to get sacked for burning the meat or a similar infraction. So we are constantly running out of tea, sugar, toilet paper, and, worst of all, filtered water. The good thing is that the present cook has started making bread at the sisters' place. Everything is bearable if you have bread. And the mango season is starting.

Mangoes in Lofilanyi village, on the Dito plateau

SIXTH LETTER

A teacher crisis

April 2013... We advertise for staff on Radio Bakhita... The deputy headmaster is sick... The death of Bishop Akio... An orphaned duiker... A ban on shooting arrows in the compound... Walking to Lofilanyi... The wandering players.

The three late-coming teachers never arrived, and well into the term we had no one to teach science except the accounts teacher, who stood in for the maths and physics teachers. The chemistry teacher left back in December with a collection of illnesses that included malaria, typhoid, amoebiasis and pneumonia. The last phone call we had from him, he said he had yellow fever too. He is still aiming to report for duty. But I wonder.

However, the medical staff, including the doctors from the hospital, have again come to our aid and are coming to the school to teach chemistry, physics, biology, physics and maths. Plus a local second year student from the University of Juba is teaching maths and physics in Senior Four (it's his long vacation). He is proving to be a wonderful teacher. The students seem to be enjoying maths for the first time. Each time I go in to a classroom I see a knot of students doing problems on the blackboard. Meanwhile the head teacher went to the Ministry of

Education in Torit to see who they had on their lists. They were as unhelpful as he predicted that they would be. The head teacher hates bureaucracy. But he would happily walk forty kilometers to Ikotos and back to get some errand done. I wrote an advertisement for teachers which was broadcast on Radio Bakhita (the Catholic Church Radio) and friends have put it on notice boards in Torit and Juba, where there are said to be many unemployed teachers. The advert stresses that the post would suit those who like a rural environment.

The deputy head has been sick most of the term. I saw him in hospital yesterday, so I know he is not malingering. I have taken over his history classes – East African History (the Coastal trade and then the missionaries) and Sudan History (colonialism and resistance to it). This is a joy, although it means my timetable is now quite full.

The big event here has been the death of Bishop Akio of Torit, which means that the diocese is without a bishop. I met Bishop Akio when he came to stay here; he was a good, simple man, very easy to get on with. I noted his gift for recruiting people like Charles the Engineer in airports and Indian hospitals. Charles, like many others he was in contact with, then became totally devoted to him, prepared to work unstintingly for little money. His death may have been hastened by a crisis in the diocese. The vicar-general was dismissed more than a year ago for embezzling funds. And it is said that other employees of the diocese had gone so far as to copy the bishop's seal and imitate his signature and then try to escape in a land cruiser with dollars and equipment. They were brought back from the Ugandan border to Torit but then released. I doubt anyone will be held accountable. Not that Bishop Akio was implicated in any of this. They found only 2 dollars and 150 Kenyan shillings in his rooms after he died.

But after these scandals were revealed the projects were taken away from the diocese and given to Caritas Torit. The bishop had a nine-hour closed meeting with the priests of the diocese. And then it seems he stopped bothering to eat.

Father Ben, the bishop's secretary, himself had pneumonia at the time. He struggled back to Torit two weeks ago and took the bishop to hospital in Juba, carrying US $2,000 for expenses. They would not treat Bishop Akio without receiving the money in advance in South Sudanese pounds. The bishop had to wait two hours while Father Ben rushed around trying to change money. Then all the consultant said was that the bishop would need to be seen in Nairobi. So they used the rest of the money to buy plane tickets.

In Nairobi, the Aga Khan Hospital demanded US $2,500 before they would look at the bishop. So again the bishop had to wait, this time for five hours, while Father Ben looked for money, eventually using the credit card of an American priest he had met in the plane. So the bishop was finally admitted. But he died that night. The official cause of death was heart failure. (The story of being turned away from the hospitals for lack of money is not confidential; it was broadcast over the radio in an interview with Father Ben.)

A small duiker was brought to the compound by a hunter who had shot its mother. I called her Joanna as my friend Joanna was due to visit me that day. We fed her on milk through a hospital syringe. She survived, and now she is eating greens, onion skins, and ugali (maize porridge). She butts everyone's legs and sniffs up women's skirts, perhaps looking for teats. She is not exactly fraternising with the other animals in the compound – the ducks, the chickens, the cat and the dog – but she's living in peace with them.

There used to be two cats, but one day I saw the watchmen and Franco the orphan gathering round the grandmother cat, trying to shoot it using a bow and fearsome-looking arrows, because it had killed two chicks. They were whooping with excitement. Maybe it was something to do with the death of the Bishop. (A general breakdown of law and order used to follow the death of a pope.) But I declared shooting in the compound banned and insisted that the cat be killed painlessly.

One day I climbed to the village of Lofilanyi in Dito, a high plateau where Anyanya rebels had a base in the first Sudanese civil war, in the 1960s. Lovely. Since I've walked about so much many people knew me – "Ah, Elizabeth, we met you on the river bank!". There didn't seem to be a separation between the people living on the mountain and the villages at the foot. In nearly every household the wife – or sometimes the husband – came from the valley below. In Lofilanyi I found an excellent potter and a thumb piano player. In Loyei, a woman catechist. There was a school with two teachers. They have no help from the state nor from the diocese and set their own exams and give their own certificates. They had three blackboards, one classroom and benches of bamboo. They were teaching Primary One under a tree.

We didn't stay the night in Dito. I wanted to get back as a group of wandering players was coming on Sunday. Actually they had turned up in the Parish Compound on the previous day without warning (as everyone does since there are no phones) aiming to perform for International Women's Day. But it rained all morning and they left, promising to come back on Sunday. They were from Manna Sudan, a community-based organisation based in Ikwoto, the county centre of Ikotos. They explained to Sister Paskwina that they suited their plays to the problems of the area. They could perform plays on violence, cattle raiding, alcoholism, forced marriage, compensation, domestic violence, inheritance, and negligence. Sister P. told them: "We have all those things". As it was for Women's Day they did plays on forced marriage and giving girls as compensation, that is giving a girl from your family to another family if one of your family has killed someone from that family.

A dozen of our students were sitting on logs waiting for them to begin. Manna Sudan were late starting and I saw them pulling a couple of their actors away from nearby bars. But within five minutes there were a hundred spectators, mostly children, and by the end of the first play, about 300.

Tartisio Abuna, a teacher at St Augustine's School (standing),
with his father, Lucio Ohia

SEVENTH LETTER

Incidents at St Augustine's

May 2013... A student attacks a teacher... The head boy
suffers tribal abuse... A girl is beaten by her relatives...
The Italian teachers organize a film show... The village
where no men are left alive.

L ast term was the first time at Isohe School that we didn't
have to end early from lack of food, so perhaps we are
getting on a firmer foundation. Sorghum from the school
garden lasted a month this term and there will be plenty of cassava
next term. There are more pupils this year – over a hundred more
than last year – but that also means there is more fee income for
the school to use. There have been a number of violent incidents,
though: one student punched a teacher and was expelled. The
man he punched was Ambrose, the CRE teacher. That is to say,
Christian Religious Education.

Ambrose is a former child soldier and a Dongotono, as is the
boy who punched him, and they are distantly related. After a
week in hospital in Ikotos, Ambrose came back and – correctly,
I thought – asked the head to forgive the boy who had hit him.
The head – correctly again, I thought – refused. I spoke at
length to the boy, advising him to count to ten first in future.
He'll be going to the secondary school in Ikotos now. We won't

be sponsoring him anymore, so he will have to find the money.

There were other acts of violence. The head boy, who comes from Central Equatoria, suffered tribal abuse. A girl was beaten by two boys, her relatives. Other students apparently looked on and didn't intervene. The head teacher told me that he was going to beat the culprits in front of the whole school and then expel them. They were expelled, but I don't know about the beating. Another girl was kicked by a boy, again a relative. Such incidents didn't happen last year. Robert, the library prefect, says he thinks many of these antagonisms start with food: either prefects give large helpings and it runs out, angering people, or they give small helpings and the complaint is of tribalism or favouritism.

There are two Italian teachers here from AVSI, the Italian educational NGO. One of the teachers, Gabriele, is a footballer, a good role model. He thought that the incidents of violence were related to the lack of recreational activities and clubs at the school. A Ugandan colleague said that his school in Uganda had a Christian students' society, an AIDS group, a Literary Club, several sports clubs and a drama club. Here we only have football and Scrabble (only a few play Scrabble). The chess and draughts have disappeared.

So G. started a film-showing each Saturday, at the hospital. He faced difficulties, though, from the head teacher, who said that the students would pick up infections at the hospital. (This is ridiculous, as students go to the hospital every day.) Or else, the head said, they would slip away for the night. (This is equally ridiculous, as the school has no wall, so that it is perfectly easy for students to slip out for the night anyway, as one senior girl did recently.)

The first film G. showed was Mel Gibson's *The Passion of the Christ*. This was on Good Friday; only thirteen listed students were allowed to go. Then he showed one of the *Chronicles of Narnia* and *Shrek*. He stressed the Christian allegory, but didn't let me know in time for me to prepare a explanation for the students. In Narnia the students saw snow and trains, and ogres. (The last actually crop up on the English syllabus, in folktales.) I suggested that a better alternative might be films about Africa or made in Africa, such as *Biko*. But G. has his own ideas. Anyway, as a result of the burst of student violence we had to suspend films at the end of last term. We had a formal meeting with the head teacher and it was agreed that they would be a normal occurrence on Saturday evenings next term. G. means to start with *ET*. What with *ET*, *Shrek*, *The Passion of the Christ* and *Narnia* these kids, few of whom have seen films before, will get a strange idea of life in western countries.

For the first time, in April, they put me on joint 24-hour supervision duty with my colleague Lucy, who teaches commerce. I don't think anyone thought I would be very serious. They just thought that I should earn my US $250-equivalent pay-check by taking part.

"OK. No beating", I said to Lucy. I read aloud to her the transitional constitution of South Sudan, which prohibits beating in schools. This clause was, of course, clearly inserted by wimpish foreign human rights advisers. All the teachers beat misbehaving students, and the kids don't complain. So I don't make waves about it. But I do get tired of being told "we Africans learn through our buttocks". In my first day of duty L. pulled a group of students out of Assembly for some serious crime like wearing sandals. I gave up and escaped to the staff room. I could hear the thwacking of the cane. It merged with the sound of an axe felling trees in the distance. One or the other continued for the next hour, a sign of my powerlessness either to save the environment or the students. I suggested that we should have a rule that only a woman teacher can beat a girl-student. Everyone seemed astonished.

The other common form of punishment is gardening. Sister Paskwina says teachers prefer beating because they are too lazy to supervise gardening. I complained that students were right outside my classroom being punished by cutting grass. "Can't you at least punish them in their free time?" I said. "But that wouldn't be a punishment", said the teacher on duty.

How different this place is from schools in Europe! Left by the teacher to copy notes or do exercises the class remains totally silent. Or if the teacher has given them nothing to do one of them takes over teaching. For the first term exams, the teacher would write the exam on the board and leave the class to it, with an apparent certainty that there would be no cheating.

After the elopement of one of our sponsored students, L., the Commerce teacher, and myself have been interviewing every one of the 36 girls in the school to see if there were any others in danger of leaving because of marriage, forced or unforced, or parental antagonism to education. Twenty of these have lost their fathers, six of them by shooting. The first day we interviewed them about their families, their preferred subjects and what they wanted to do when they left. But we felt we were not getting enough information about whether they were in danger of being taken out of school to be married.

So L. began to quiz them quite aggressively: "We know that among your people they marry girls off early, at the age of twelve or thirteen" she would say. "Will that not happen to you? What if your brother needs the cows for a wife? Will you not leave to get married? Every girl said they wanted to continue, but many one feared for. If they were from Acholi, they might insist "No, our people leave a girl till she is eighteen...." If not, we would have to push further and say "What will you do in your village when all your friends are married and you aren't and they are abusing you for being old and not married?". One of them hung her head and said, "They are already abusing me", in an almost inaudible voice. We fear she will not stay long at school.

Sometimes one of the girls would protest strongly and wonderfully. "No, I am not even thinking like that," said one. Another said "No, if a millionaire comes for me I will not accept him". And another: "They are already abusing me and I don't mind". A girl from a very remote village said: "When my mother said that I should marry, I said to her: 'My mother, send me to school, I don't have a father, I don't have brothers, I don't have sisters. You are crying but I must continue. Here there is not even a good hospital, the people are suffering, and no boy from our village has finished school. I will be a doctor or a nurse'".

We would press them also on how they would find the money; a supportive father was the most important thing, but mothers were more likely to be supportive (and many of the girls had lost their fathers). Uncles, cousins and brothers might be good or negligent. Many spoke of the difficulties: "Money is not there," they would say. "Hunger is there".

AVSI, the Italian NGO, only pays half school fees as they think that able-bodied young people should be sufficiently motivated to earn the other half of the cost. Obviously the way one would like people to get money is by selling crops, but the easiest way for a boy to earn money is by chopping trees for firewood, and for a girl the best way is by brewing alcohol (custom dictates that men can't do this). Ten girls named alcohol-brewing as a way they or their mothers got their school fees. I asked AVSI whether, by giving only half-scholarships, they were not increasing alcoholism and, consequently, deaths by gunshot in Sudan. They said that this policy of paying only a half fee was set as the plan for the next three years.

For our own sponsored students, I have given full scholarships for next term, since May is the planting month. Apart from selling cassava, which is ripe now, it is more difficult to get money at that time. and I thought students should spend the month helping in the farm. But I warned them that we would only pay half fees for the third term, when students should be able to harvest what they planted in May. (Since then, I've heard that there the vital May rains haven't arrived and the ground is too hard for planting).

Encouraging schoolgirls to make alcohol seems to be a problem in a country with so many alcohol problems. My language teacher, a Dongotono, said "Dongotono have no respect for life, including their own", and told me another story of killings of two weeks ago, of two brothers who, quarrelling over livestock, shot each other's cows. Following that, the younger brother shot the older and a friend shot the younger one in revenge. Three people have told me there is a village in the mountains where there are only women, where no men are left alive. But no one could remember the name. So I think it may be a Dongotono myth.

I hope this drought won't destroy everyone's plans. Thanks to Father Ben – now finally confirmed as our new parish priest – and Mama Magdalene and the project they call "Women's Empowerment for Peace and Agricultural Security", Isohe is in the vanguard when it comes to empowering women in agriculture, peace-building and literacy. After months of work the diocesan mechanic, Michael – who studied agricultural mechanics in Denmark, and has refused good offers of work elsewhere with higher pay – got an old Italian-donated tractor going. When I had left he had already ploughed the parish land. And we had a lovely ten days when an Ethiopian from UNESCO and a Dinka from the Ministry of Education led a workshop to train adult literacy teachers, who will focus on women. More on that later, but they were both great people, and we had a week of interesting late-night discussions. That is the good thing about the fathers' house. Nice people come to stay. And the television is broken.

Preparing a lesson, St Kizito's Primary School

EIGHTH LETTER

Happiness and drunkardness

June 2013... Nuba students plant seed instead of paying fees... A diary writing project... Building a house for the rainmaker... An anti-corruption meeting attracts few attendees... Happiness and drunkardness.

The mechanic, Michael, drove our newly repaired tractor from Narus to here, a distance of over 100 miles. The vast lands at Lolit, fifteen kilometers away, which are earmarked partly for the women's empowerment project, are still not ploughed. The second planting season begins in July, next month, so it is unlikely that anything will happen this year. However, just as I was leaving at the beginning of May, Michael was able to plough about eighteen acres of the parish land between the slopes and the Awali stream, and then about six acres belonging to the school. And Father Ben and the head teacher decided to use our Nuba students, refugees from the fighting up north in Sudan, to plant the land in lieu of payment of their school fees.

There are six Nuba boys in our school and fourteen girls studying at St Matthew's (another diocesan school) in Ikotos. As far as I can find out, this was another project of the late Bishop Akio, and the elusive Bishop of El Obeid. When Bishop Akio died there were no funds for the project, so Father Ben gathered all the girls to stay in the Parish compound (where there is a complex of thatched huts to sleep in) and all were put to pay their way by planting maize on the parish land.

I gave Senior Three a diary project and learnt a lot about what happened during the holidays. On the last day of school, one of them recorded that the head teacher had warned them against cattle-raiding. *"It was on the morning of the last day of closing,"* he wrote. *"Headmaster was addressing students that whenever you go you behave well let you come back to school do not go to cattle-raiding as long as you are a student do not do that."* Then, he added, with a fine sense of irony, *"Immediately at the same day for some minute the student took the gun from his parent and shot his youngest brother. He was arrested by Police he was beaten."*

Reading the students' diaries I learned that a local man had fallen off a tractor and injured his leg on the disc blades; that a head teacher had a fight with his wife; and that at a meeting with MPs about cattle-raiding and corruption, few people had shown up. *"When people refuse to come to the meeting,"* one of the students noted, *"the Chief of Isohe send police to collect people within the village to come for meeting by Force."* *"Although they Force still Few people,"* he added. And when police chased the women from the market, they fled with their children on their backs *"like Jesus chasing people selling from the temple"*.

When I came back to Isohe there had been no rain for a month. An article in the Senior Three newspaper was headlined "Isohe Community believe in rainmaker". Magisto, the reporter, related how, on 3 May, the local rainmaker denied that it was God, the Creator of Heaven and Earth, who made rain. He was reported to have said "if you want rain let the community of Isohe contribute something that can make me feel happy". At his demand, they built him a house. Each household, Magisto informed us, contributed "five South Sudanese pounds, two cups of sorghum, tobacco and even the goat" to the rainmaker's housebuilding. On 2 June, when there was still no rain he said "Wait for three days". On 6 June, the article reported, the rain came.

Among those who sought out the rainmaker, going up to the holy place on the mountain in Dito, was one of our catechists. Father C, on the other hand, revealed that he had prayed to God for rain at Mass on that Sunday. So who knows who should take the credit. Since then there has been plenty of rain. Too much, in fact. A storm – rain and thunder and lightning and large hailstones and strong winds – blew the top right off my colleague Lucy's house. It blew down the school kitchen (a corrugated iron shack) and lifted off the roof of the front room of the priest's apartment right next to mine. Then it replaced it again! We had to hang every piece of paper out to dry, and I oversaw the clearing out and washing of the room that lost its roof. It was striking that, as far as I could see, none of the local mud-walled thatched huts was damaged.

Senior Four carried out a job satisfaction project. They found out that everyone in Isohe was pretty happy (that is to say they listed more causes of happiness than unhappiness). The farmer said it was nice feeding the family with your own food, hard when there was drought. The school cook said it was nice feeding children and bringing money home (she only gets about US $30 a month), but hard when the pay didn't come. The trader said it was nice making profits only the roads were bad and it was difficult to get goods to Isohe. An NGO officer from AVSI couldn't find anything to complain about in his job. He said that even setbacks were learning opportunities. He was clearly well-taught in NGO thinking. All teachers and school workers said the main thing wrong was the delay in salaries. We are still waiting for our salaries for May.

Many students write of "drunkardness", I correct their spelling, but they have obviously been taught to write it that way. And what's wrong with it? It's perfectly understandable. In fact it can happily coexist with "drunkenness" to mean the next step towards alcoholism.

I missed the peak of the mango season. For a week during the holiday the Nuba students said they were eating fifty a day as there was no other food. Then they ended. After two weeks without mangoes, people started bringing them down from the mountains. Many don't eat them, saying they are sour, but they are fine and very cheap. The cabbage season hasn't started yet, so we are still eating mainly beans.

School assembly at St Kizito's Primary School

NINTH LETTER

Death and the tractor

September 2013... A man falls from a cassia tree... Roast pork...
The pet duiker dies... The feasts of the church... The wily
Combonis... The European Union... A near-death experience...
On a quinine drip... Eating a chapati.

A man called Luka climbed a cassia tree in the parish
grounds to cut branches to sell, having taken five or
six sachets of the strong alcohol they sell here called
"Empire". Drunk, he fell to his death. The family claimed compensation, but three witnesses confirmed that between his
accident and his death Luka had told them no one should be
held liable for his death. The judge in Ikotos agreed. So justice
was done. The person who had been pushing for compensation
was the brother of the deceased. He had himself killed one of
his other brothers in a drunken quarrel five years before. Did he
pay compensation then? Not being an anthropologist it took me
some time to realise that this would be a completely different
kind of case: you don't pay compensation for killing your own
brother because their family becomes part of your responsibility.
And you can't pay compensation to yourself.

At the fathers' compound where I live we now have three pigs;
Father Ben was talking a few months ago of how much he loved

roast pork. Accordingly, he celebrated the fifth anniversary of his ordination with a roast pork party, thrown by the hospital staff. Myself and Mama Magdalene, the women's organiser, who has been spending more time here lately, are a good deal less keen on these pigs. They are really not beautiful; and the compound is beginning to smell like a farmyard. Each morning, after the rain, I wake up to find the earth of this religious house criss-crossed with prints of cloven hooves.

Some time ago the pet duiker, Joanna, died after days of refusing to eat. They said she ate something poisonous, or that she caught pneumonia. I tried to coax her to eat, but to no avail. In the morning of the fourth day, Franco said "Joanna died in the night". I stroked her body and said: "Now we have to dig a hole for her grave and bury her". Franco looked at me astonished: "Should we not rather give her to the *mzee* [Swahili for old man] outside the gate to eat?" "Of course we should", I said, quickly changing tack. There's been another duiker since then. Mama M. gave him milk, but I didn't have time to name him or bond with him before he, too, died.

Life is punctuated with the feasts of the State, or of the Church. There is Independence Day followed by Martyrs' Day (which comes rather too soon after and is under-celebrated as people are jaded), then the Feast of the Assumption. And soon there will be the ceremony for the hanging of the bells and the Feast of St Teresa on 1 October. The new bells – which are not so beautiful as the old cracked ones, which have inscriptions and reliefs of religious scenes – are the gift of the congregation of the Church of St Teresa in Varese, near Milan. The hanging of the bells will be attended by the priest and representatives of the Varese parish. The latter will have to get back in time to celebrate St Teresa's day in Varese.

How people love a feast! Church or State, the organisation tends to be similar. A three-hour Mass, in the case of the religious festivals, followed by a wait outside the Church for food, which is served first to dignitaries and then to as many village people as it will go round – at least a couple of hundred and maybe as many as five hundred. In the midst of constant financial crises money always seems to be found for feasts. The feast of the Assumption was striking as they killed two bulls and gave one to the primary and secondary school students, whose diet never normally includes meat – in fact never anything but porridge and beans.

The entertainment is always pretty much the same. There are the Children of the Infant Jesus, singing uplifting songs that they make up themselves, the choir from the secondary school, doing the same, the Woroworo women dancers, and, finally, the primary school scout troop, dressed in khaki with caps, giving displays of stamping and leaping. All this is interspersed with speeches from the village chief, the parish priest, the head teacher, the headmistress of the primary school, the woman's representative, the youth representative, and sometimes the commissioner. If we're lucky the school drama group will put on a play, but they didn't the last two times. On both those feasts it rained heavily. When festivities resumed everything was mud. The boy scouts slipped and fell as they were performing (I'm afraid one of them fractured a leg). Yet, after a delay of two hours due to the rain and the wait for food there were still a thousand or so people – mostly children – waiting to watch and cheer. They even cheered the speeches.

Meanwhile the school farm at Lolit has been getting underway. The money from the European Union, which was supposed to come in January, finally arrived at the beginning of August.

This was just at the end of the season, when both schools were sitting exams. Sister P. said there was no way she could keep the primary school pupils in school once the exams were finished, but in the secondary school they would have to stay to get their report cards. So we started and finished exams early and during the last week of term the tractor carried twenty boys a day to the farm and we started clearing the land. It is a wonderful project – aiming to provide food to feed the primary and secondary school so that we don't run out each term as we have in the past. If you think about it, the money the school receives from all pupils' school fees – supposing they are all paid – comes to about 5,000 euros a term. From this the school pays for food and equipment and salaries for any staff not registered with the Ministry of Education. (The students have to provide their own exercise books, pens and even paper for writing their exams on). So the 61,000 euros from the EU would give the secondary school complete ease for four years. As for land, the secondary school already has eleven acres in the valley, and for the first time this year we got it all planted with cassava. All the land, whoever farms it, up as far as a landmark cassia tree two kilometers away, is parish land, thanks to the wily Comboni Fathers.

The land at Lolit is fifteen kilometers away. We have the tractor for the moment, but later the pupils will have to walk it. Charles has nearly finished building a galvanised metal store there for seeds and tools. The land is being planted with cassava as it is late in the season and anything else will be uprooted by monkeys or wild pigs. They are going to pay for three watchmen to guard the land in shifts all the year, since cassava takes a year before harvesting.

I asked the head teacher: "Won't that eat up all the profits?" He said, "Yes". I told Richard Oyet, who got the grant, that I failed to see the economics of it, except that the EU seem to like the idea of giving money in order to make schools self-sustaining, while thinking, for some reason, that paying for labs, textbooks or teachers is not their role. He agreed.

Between the beginning of writing this letter and the ending of it, I had something like a near-death experience, the result of the engrained feeling our generation seems to have that you shouldn't disturb doctors except in direst need. During the week I had fever and went to the hospital, but no clinician was on duty, so I said I would come back on Monday. Robert Somali, the clinician from the malaria program came out of hours and gave me malaria drugs but I still wasn't convinced it was malaria and only started taking them on Saturday. Then I must have fallen unconscious.

I woke up in a room on a quinine drip surrounded by anxious people. The head girl and another student slept on the floor by my bed all night saying "Tea? Porridge?" or giving me Panadol. But on Monday afternoon, the clinician agreed to discharge me. It was like taking up my bed and walking. My sheets, blanket, pillow and crockery more than filled three basins carried on the heads of the girls. The hospital room where I had been was emptied, only the bed and table remained.

I asked everyone what had happened. "You were found", said Sister P. "By whom?" "By me. I found you," she said. "It was 8.30. Then Richard carried you down by car". Later I asked the head teacher the same question. But his answer was different. "Richard found you on the floor of your room at 10.30," he said. At this point I remembered how, when I was a student at the Centre for West African Studies back in Britain, we would consider multiple accounts of a single incident and try to work out the reasons for the variations. And I remembered how later, at

Amnesty International, when I was working on the Middle East, we would do the opposite: try and establish a single truth. We had to do this, because if we said, for example, that an event happened at 8 AM instead of 10 AM the Israeli government would jump on us and say all our information was clearly false.

In the present case perhaps it doesn't really matter what is true. In fact the different stories I think I am hearing about my collapse may all be a result of the fact that quinine distorts your hearing. It makes everyone sound like a 33 rpm vinyl record played at 45 rpm. Today, in any case, I am well enough to eat a chapati with Charles before he goes to Lolit. So I ask him "Why didn't you check that that I was alive on Sunday morning?" "But I did!" he says. "It was I who came to your door at 7.30 and found you!"

Mother and child in Isohe.

TENTH LETTER

Guava thieves

November 2013... Two students fall pregnant... Speaking
the vernacular... I remain silent... Threats of expulsion...
Sheets, mattresses, jerrycans and gumboots... A plastic
chair... Hoes and slashers... How to stop guava thieves.

At the beginning of term two students turned out to be
pregnant. One was a sponsored student of ours. She
wouldn't tell me, though it was obvious. Later she wrote
me a letter admitting it. Sister Paskwina was the one who had
asked us to sponsor her. "She has a brain," Sister P. said, "and
her father said there was no point in sponsoring girls. He said it
was better to marry them off early and not risk losing the bride
wealth. Now he will be saying 'I told you so'." I was afraid her
father would beat her. But neither Sister Paskwina nor Mama
Magdalene thought it was worthwhile intervening. Luckily her
father lives twelve kilometers away, so I gave the student the
money to go to the secondary school in Ikotos, twenty kilometers
in the opposite direction. Perhaps she avoided seeing her father
altogether.

The other pregnant student was the wonderful S., producer
of our school dramas. The last drama she produced, for the wel-
coming of Senior One and introduction of new prefects in July,

was about teachers who seduced schoolgirls. This was rather close to the bone in the case of one of the teachers – he married a student last term. Both this term's pregnant students had affairs not with teachers but with drivers, one from AVSI, the Italian NGO, and one from the hospital. This is significant. Drivers are a part of the small mobile population round here that enjoys a good income; they are therefore likely to have a wife in several towns. I pointed out to the head teacher that, because of the lack of girls in education, South Sudan educational regulations state that no girl should be penalised for pregnancy. But he just said "They will disturb the other girls". So I sent my student to St Matthew's Girls Secondary at Ikotos, and advised AVSI to do the same for the other one. Then they can come back to school in Isohe once the babies are born.

L. and I tried to hold a discussion about this with all the girls in the school, but it didn't really work. They didn't talk much. There is a certain cliquishness among them, involving talking in their own languages, so that outsiders don't understand. The head girl, who comes from another part of the state, complains about this. In theory, speaking in vernacular is forbidden in the school (except me, when I am trying to learn it). There used to be an awful custom that involved those caught not speaking English having to carry a chicken's head on a string; the culprit could only get rid of it by passing it on to someone else who had committed the same offence.

There are lots of rules I don't know till they are broken; and threats of expulsion are frequent. Father Ben harangued the primary school in Church one day last term saying they weren't coming to church and every single student who failed to come to church would be expelled from school. Coming out of Mass I said to Mama M. "I'm not sure that it would be legal to expel

900 students for not coming to church". She said, quite indignantly, "A parish priest can do what he likes in his own parish". In the same way, when I said to the head teacher that he couldn't expel a pregnant girl, he replied: "I can do what I like in my own school." I don't fight this. One of my Dongotono teacher Elizabeth's favourite phrases, whenever anything outrageous occurred, was "*Abuho nang*", which means "I remained silent". It is a good precept. The Sunday after Father Ben's pronouncement the Church was packed with primary school children, though I doubt if all 1,000 were there. Last Sunday we were back to normal, with scarcely a hundred.

Two terms ago every student was ordered to bring a long list of things: sheets, mattress, ten-liter jerrycan, gumboots and a plastic chair. About ten students brought gumboots and two a plastic chair. Last term the headmaster's letter – which I type out for him – demanded that every student bring a hoe and a slasher for clearing long grass. At the beginning of this term the head teacher refused to register students who had failed to bring them, and sent them home. Curiously, you can buy slashers in Isohe, but not hoes. There are blacksmiths among the Dongotono and you can buy hoes in the mountains. But in the small villages up there you can't buy slashers (why would you want to?). So you can't get both things in one place, even if you can afford them. It seemed to me – and to the students – particularly unfair that Senior Four students, with only one term left to go, had to turn back and comb the country, borrowing, begging and perhaps stealing, to find hoes. One of our students in Senior Four had arrived early as I said that no late-arriving student would get sponsorship; then he had to walk back the thirty kilometers to his home in Iloli to borrow a hoe and slasher. Like Father Ben, the head threatens more expulsions than he actually carries out.

Many who beg me for school fees say "and we couldn't pay last term" and I find it is true, even though a month into the term everyone with unpaid fees was threatened with expulsion.

And a word about the thieves. There are cassava thieves, and maize thieves (they come from a local village), and guava thieves, mostly girls (I feel sympathetic). I am glad to say that the Parish on the whole uses a good kind of punishment: those who are caught have to cultivate a *katala* (a ten by twenty meter strip of land) for the parish, and two *katala* of cassava or maize for themselves, all this to be inspected so they shouldn't have to steal again. One was caught by the watchman and locked in the parish store for the head teacher to deal with. As the head was interviewing her in the compound, her brother, who is in Senior Three, came running up and pulled a kitchen knife on the Head; everyone stood frozen to the spot till he put it away. I'd have thought that would be an expellable offence, yet the boy has come back to school.

An elderly priest, Father John Baptist, in semi-retirement in Ikotos has come to be assistant parish priest with us. He is passionate about gardens, nurseries and planting, and he said that he put a stop to guava stealing by giving each primary school child two seedlings to take home, so every home would have their own guavas.

Father Ben took the night bus from Kampala and arrived just in time for Mass on 1 November. It's the following day, though – 2 November, All Souls' Day – that is the more important date in the calendar. I believe that it was popular pressure in the eleventh century that elevated this celebration of the faithful dead to its present status. Here in Isohe the cemetery was cleared of grass so you could actually see the two cement graves and the small chapel with a stone commemorating a Brother Malotti who died of blackwater fever around 1933.

Father Ben preached a sermon. He started by saying that Dongotono don't like thinking of death. Even the choir didn't like to practise funeral songs. "How many of you believe in the resurrection of the dead?" he asked. There was only a murmur. Then he went on to say: «We Dongotono traditionally believe in a sort of afterlife. For example, the crocodile and the monkey clans think they will be reborn as crocodiles or monkeys". In fact, though, he said, the reality is better. People would not be reborn as crocodiles or monkeys, but, he warned the congregation, unlike the saints who walk straight into heaven without hesitation, we would all go to purgatory.

"What is purgatory?" asked Father Ben. "We have all been refugees," he continued. "Remember how, before you even got to the refugee settlement, you would spend time just waiting in a half-way camp? So purgatory is a half-way camp on the way to heaven. You have no control over your own destiny, you just have to wait. You can't make appeals, so we who are outside are the ones to make appeals on behalf of those inside."

On All Souls' Day, he said priests should say at least three masses. And all of us should call into the Church every hour to pray for people's souls. Then Father Ben deployed another image, more sectarian, about the journey to heaven. He said that during his night bus trip from Kampala the conductor told them: "At the mid-way stop in the bus station get out but don't drink too much. There are lots of buses and you might get on the wrong one and end up in Gulu or Lira instead of Kitgum." In life, said Father Ben, there were many buses that went in the wrong direction, and if you did not take care you could end getting onto a Protestant bus, or a Salafi bus, instead of a good Catholic bus.

Armed youth in Eastern Equatoria

ELEVENTH LETTER

Ghost teachers, scorpions. broken chairs

December 2013... The cattle-raiding exam... The murder of the school carpenter... Broken chairs go unrepaired... Official languages in South Sudan... Ghost teachers... Next tomorrow.

The subject of the Comprehension test in the school certificate exam this year was cattle-raiding. Cattle-raiding is a specialty round here, so it was much easier for the students than last year's test, when the subject was the fifth and seventh Pan-African Congress. A Ministry of Education directive apparently says that no students should be present in the school at the time of the school certificate exams, except for those taking the exam. Or maybe it's because the teachers want to go home. Or because each school certificate candidates needs a desk and chair to themselves and there aren't enough to go round. (In fact there aren't even enough chairs for the teachers. We sit on a fallen tree trunk, half-eaten by termites.)

The problem is that neither desks or chairs have been getting mended since the school carpenter was murdered by his drunken nephews. No action was taken against the nephews. They are his closest relatives and any compensation would have to be paid back to them. For the same reason the nephews were not arrested by the police. Or perhaps it was because the police were afraid of them. Last week, though, one nephew was found stabbed to death. And the other one has become very thin, they say, because his strength is sapped by supernatural powers.

I am lucky to be free of malaria this term, having been provided with prophylactics by E. Practically everyone else here has been hospitalised at some point. And unfortunately the staff of the hospital have not been paid for six months. So they left *en masse* for Torit to complain, leaving the hospital without staff for two days. Then the hospital ran out of anti-malaria drugs, except for amodiaquine, which has the worst side-effects of all. And one of the lab technicians left and the other went on leave. So for nearly a month they couldn't do lab tests.

For the first time since I came here we have had two Muslims visiting the Parish. One is a Fellata, the descendent of a follower of Osman dan Fodio who migrated in the nineteenth century from West Africa and settled in al-Fasher, in Darfur, and whose father moved from there to Wau. He arrived here with Mama Magdalene's son; they both studied at Ahlia University in Khartoum. They are journalists and plan to establish a history magazine to be called Heritage. These two young people believe, remarkably, in eventual Sudanese reunification – to follow revolutions in Sudan and South Sudan. The other Muslim visitor is the Ministry of Education Examinations Monitor, who teaches Arabic and Islamic Religious Education. These subjects do not figure in the South Sudan School Certificate. But in fact three of the ten states in South Sudan have kept to the Sudanese Arabic school certificate from the old Sudan. These states present no students for the new School Certificate.

It's ridiculous, really, that Arabic has not been made the second official language of South Sudan, since everybody here speaks it – either Juba Arabic or Sudanese Arabic – and generally in preference to English. Arabic is the language used when commissioners or priests want to be sure that people understand what they say. In St Kizito Primary School they solve the problem by treating Arabic as the mother tongue – i.e. the language of instruction to be used in the first three years of school.

This is my last term teaching here in Isohe. So I will be saying goodbye not just to South Sudan, but also to Sudanese English. This year's Letter to Parents (which I did not edit this time) reports that three boys were dismissed and three girls "dismissed themselves by fornication and pregnancy". (I hope they undismiss themselves too.) The commonest words in use to describe uncooperative students are "stubborn" and "dodging". In fact "stubborn" is used as a general term of criticism in South Sudan. For instance, the Dinka, largest single ethnic group in the country, are often described by non-Dinka as "stubborn". It is a pity there are no Dinka in the school so the students can judge for themselves. In Isohe as a whole there is only one Dinka, a shop owner with a local Dongotono wife.

I explained to Senior Three the other day that in English as spoken in England there was no such expression as "next tomorrow" (the standard South Sudanese English expression for " the day after tomorrow"). They could hardly believe it. I also told them that since English is the official language of South Sudan, once they have passed their school certificate they can make of it what they like and that they should feel free to use "next tomorrow", if they want. And "footing" for walking – and any other expression they choose.

I am happy to say there is much less beating in the school now. We had two workshops in the past year emphasising that the practice was now outlawed. In one school assembly, though, a new teacher caned a boy who had dodged his class. The boy's nickname – he's proud of it – is Yau Yau, after the South Sudanese rebel leader who has been causing mayhem in Jonglei State. After a stroke of the cane he leapt up laughing.

At least we didn't run out of food at the school this year. There was not enough extra money, though, to top up teachers' salaries. Under the Memorandum with the Diocese, teachers in faith schools like ours are paid by the Ministry of Education. But a teacher doesn't get on the Ministry books until the calendar year after they start. Thus I arrived in January 2012, and during the first year received just a couple of handouts – two hundred South Sudan pounds a time (about US $45). After a teacher has left their post, on the other hand, the Ministry tends to go on paying his or her salary for another year. The school uses the money coming to these non-existent teachers to pay other teachers who aren't on the books, or to boost existing teachers' salaries. This past year the school had two ghost salaries, but we had three teachers to be paid from this money, not to mention the hospital staff who teach science. I'd intended to inform the Ministry of Education that I was leaving at the end of this term, but the head teacher made it quite clear that I must continue as a ghost teacher. And I came to understand what a bad mistake it would have been, depriving the school of 1,000 South Sudan pounds (currently about US $225) a month. I am one of only two women teachers now. When I leave, L. will be the last. I couldn't blame her if she were to leave – she has two small children at home in Uganda, one with medical problems needing more than her monthly salary for treatment. She is thinking of going into the clothes business.

The new administration in the diocese of Torit is gradually taking action against corruption. Father Ben was proud of himself for unmasking the logistician and getting him put in prison. ("Did he think I couldn't tell the difference between a new clutch plate and a fourth-hand Chinese one costing SSP 3,000?" he asked.) But within a week, somehow, the logistician had escaped from prison.

In Isohe we have an elderly priest, Father John Baptist, with a passion for growing anything – preparing a nursery, planting seeds of pawpaws, lemons, anything – and a habit of calling the congregation "comrades", which he may have picked up from the Sudan People's Liberation Army during their socialist period in the early part of the north-south civil war. When the SPLA passed through in the early 1980s Father John would give them sweet potatoes. That was how he saved the intermediate students – including the future Bishop and three future priests – from recruitment as child soldiers. The SPLA Commander looked them over and said they were "good officer material" and should stay in the school, which was then an SPLA training centre. Notwithstanding the sweet potatoes, in 1992 Father John was put in an SPLA Prison in Kidepo camp for a hundred days, with Bishop Paride Taban, and two missionary fathers from Ireland and France, Father Leo and Father Yoana Lafasier.

The rainy season ends as the term ends. Suddenly the grass is dry and scorpions appear in houses. The weather is still pleasant, though, with a light, warm breeze, while in Torit and Juba it is becoming really hot during the day. This week the local students set off home, girls with trunks on their heads, boys mostly with backpacks, walking in groups of six or more, for safety and company.

Ten of them set out on the four-hour walk to Lobira at 4 AM. With a young person's blissful lack of understanding of physical limitations of an old *khawaja* like myself, M. urged me to come with him to his village, four hours trek through the mountains. This was to talk to his father about the history of Anyanya in the area. But walking in this season is too hard; and the heat dries the mouth up as soon as you drink. Meanwhile students who are going home to Torit or Juba – too far to walk – have to wait for vehicles which may not travel at all. Last term we had the lorry, but now it's stuck, with gear box problems.

But this is Isohe, so we are used to it. A town with no telephone network, with nothing in the market, with roads deep in mud, and a gun crime every fortnight. But with beautiful mountains, a good climate, fertile land, a strong women's group and the only undamaged church in Equatoria. And our two wondrous, struggling schools.

St Theresa's Church

TWELFTH LETTER

Government, rebels, full moon and stars

March 2015... Back in Isohe... The wind chases the rain
away... A meeting on the airstrip... Do you remember
our names?... The history of war... A dog called Omar al
Beshir... The government and the rebels... Full moon and
the brightness of stars

I'm back in Isohe, writing in the dark. It's been fifteen months since I was last here and, though Isohe hasn't been directly affected, much of the country has been plunged into civil war. I flew this time, from Juba, the capital of South Sudan, to Torit, in Eastern Equatoria. From Torit I took the road up through the hills back to the village. Surprisingly, despite the altitude, it is hotter in Isohe than Torit or Juba. It hasn't rained here yet, but tonight there was a big dust storm. They say the wind comes to chase away the rain.

On the airstrip at Torit I met Millie, a Kenyan who was studying in Khartoum when I was there in the 1970s, when we were both in our twenties. Astonishingly, after forty years, she recognised me. Millie was the eldest of thirteen children; now she is a consultant on women's reproductive rights. We remembered the time she had stayed with me in England – a frosty weekend around 1972 when we collected windfall apples off the ground and made cider. After that she and I lost touch. Four decades! It's a small place, Africa. Sometimes.

The road to Isohe was worse than I remembered; or maybe I've just become unused to the jolts. Lovely to see those mountain ranges again and to be greeted as "Elizabeth!" or "*Habboba!*" (Grandma). In Isohe there are fewer goods in the market these days. The hospital was closed for nearly a year as staff salaries were not paid. The nun administrator left; she may even have left the order. But there are two doctors now, both South Sudanese, and the hospital is open again. St Kizito's Primary School and St Augustine's Secondary School have both increased their enrolment, but there were riots at the primary school over the poor marks they got in their all-important leaving examination.

"Do you remember our names?" asks Rebecca, one of my old students. Well, I'm bad with names, but Rebecca was a memorable student. She has an unmistakeable smile that never leaves her face, whether you are teaching her the history of the Wau massacre of 1965 – when Khartoum government forces gunned down the guests at a wedding party in the town of Wau in Bahr el Ghazal – or the use of the semi-colon.

Usually, when one of the students says to me "I want to talk to you" it is a request for funds. Some students are asking if I can fund them through university in Juba. But Juba University has barely been functioning. Several of our students, including the best of the recent graduates of St Augustine's, lost two years waiting for classes to open. Now the University is open, but recently the lecturers have been on strike. Now that exams are starting students about to take exams have to work out what they should have been taught from the class outlines. And life in Juba has become very expensive. Meat there is between SSP 34 and SSP 40 a kilo (around US $10, at the official rate, more on the black market); while in Isohe it is about SSP 10 a kilo. Lecturers suffer also. They say some pack all their year's teaching into one term so that they can teach at universities elsewhere. Probably a wise strategy in a world so riven with disorder.

Here in Isohe, English and History – the subjects I taught – have suffered. The other English teacher who was here, Lokulang, got a transfer to the Ministry of Education, on a higher salary. He has been sent on a training course in Arizona, from where he sends constant emails. No one is teaching modern European history in Isohe at all. From the French Revolution to the end of the Cold War the syllabus is a blank. And with the recent collapse of the peace talks between the Government and the rebels, I have a haunting fear that all boys will be taken by the SPLA as soldiers and once again become part of their country's history of war.

The compound dogs – Mustafa and CPA – have been put down. There is another dog, not belonging to us – named Omar al Bashir after the head of state of Sudan – who has adopted the Church as his territory and lies under the pews. But the compound is still a menagerie. There are two monkeys, of different species, the smaller of them attached to the larger one, and four sows and 24 piglets. The sows have great difficulty feeding all their offspring. Until recently there were two young leopards, but they died – from eating lizards, probably. There was another duiker too – a tiny, delicate gazelle – which died, like the last one. Mama Magdalene says she refuses to take animals now, unless she knows how to look after them.

There is a new room in the compound with lots of beautiful large arched windows – part of Father Ben's scheme to enlarge the main building to be closer to the original Verona Fathers' handsome centre of the 1930s, which housed two priests and three brothers. Where did the money come from? I haven't yet asked. Meanwhile the Centre for Food Security, established to support farmers in the area, is running out of funds as there's been a dispute with Caritas Switzerland.

Lent is full of extra church services. As I arrived there was the Adoration of the Virgin. The following day I felt duty-bound to attend the 7 AM service. There were about fifty people in the congregation. Some students were caned for being late for school assembly. "Caned. And in a church school!" said Mama Magdalene. "That teacher should be transferred". I agreed. Then in the afternoon there was procession round the village, reenacting the Way of the Cross. At the Women's Centre there was supposed to be a meal cooked by men, but there was no meat in Isohe or Ikotos, and few willing men except Father Ben and the pillars of the church. In the event they came and handed out *kwete*, the local beer, and *waragi* (distilled alcohol). An hour later the women were singing and dancing in circles *"We don't want war,"* they sang. *"We are telling the government."*

When the day ends in Isohe people drop by the compound to talk, as they always did. We discuss the corruption of government, rebel advances and retreats, and whether there is a paradise. There is a full moon tonight, and, beyond and around it, the amazing brightness of stars.

Epilogue

In my first term at St Augustine's the head teacher asked me if I would consider finding sponsors for seven pupils who were unable to pay for their education. The school fees at the time were SSP 250 for full board and lodging, the equivalent of US $50 per term. It seemed to me an easy task to find seven friends who would pay the equivalent of the cost of an evening out in Europe or America in order to sponsor a deserving student in Sudan. And so it turned out to be. The project has continued to this day.

The selection of candidates is relatively straightforward. The head teacher already knows the family and home background of every student in the school. Each year those students who have not paid their fees by March are sent home to look for money; if that fails their case is considered by a committee of teachers, including the head and the director of studies. We have agreed that each student put forward for sponsoring will write me a letter, and I will allot him or her to a sponsor. Over the years the numbers have increased, but not greatly.

The sponsorship program reveals, in intimate detail, the lives and ambitions of the students – and their difficulties. When two students told me they wanted to go on to University, I encouraged them, and when they were offered places at the Catholic University of Juba, and I saw that the annual fees were under $100, I agreed to find sponsorship for them too. Now the school sponsorship scheme has expanded to include students at universities in Juba, and various health training institutes. It is a pleasure to see the joy these students take in their studies.

At the school in Isohe, the six years since I left have seen auspicious changes. When I was teaching there St Augustine's was neither the best nor the worst school in the state; its results in school certificate examinations were not outstanding. This was hardly surprising as there were no textbooks and many of the teachers were untrained. Students were not numerous: there were just over a hundred when I first arrived, and I calculated that in order to be viable the school would need at least 120, with all fees paid.

Today, six years later, the school has blossomed: it has become three times the size, with a reputation for its teaching. The greatest expansion was in 2017, the year after the fighting reached Equatoria, when the young – or some of them – chose education over joining militias and 120 students entered Senior One. And though the proportion of girls to boys has remained the same – about a third – there is less drop out than before.

There has been a spectacular improvement in examination results, in maths in particular, and in 2019 St Augustine had the highest school certificate marks in Torit State. How did this happen? At a time when teachers are still paid next to nothing, the school seems to have gathered a group of loyal and hard-working teachers (including, at last, one woman teacher, teaching English and African literature in English). On my last visit I spoke to every one of the hundred-odd students we sponsor. Many praised the teachers: "Here they are good; they care", said one. Yet the teachers are still terribly underpaid. What do they live off? Most said their gardens, or their wives, who brew and sell alcohol. One Ugandan teacher said that he grew and sold sugar-cane and bred rabbits.

(However, half the Ugandan teachers who taught at St Augustine's have left. This is because, to add to the burden of their low salaries, for the past few years officials at the South Sudanese border post have demanded that they pay a US $50 visa fee each time they crossed the border. Father Ben is said to have now persuaded the South Sudanese border officials to stop charging the fee, on the reasonable grounds that these Ugandan teachers are helping the people of South Sudan.)

Another reason for St Augustine's success is that, during the current period of uncertainty and conflict in the country, Isohe – in its hidden valley, sequestered and surrounded by mountains, and with an active priest working tirelessly for peace between communities – has remained a place of relative tranquillity. Students are coming from further and further afield – from cattle-herding communities in eastern Equatoria such as the Toposa, as well as the outlying areas of Imatong State. Jackson Lopul is still the head teacher of the school; and three local boys who studied Education in Juba University came back to teach in 2014. They now fill the positions of deputy head teacher, director of studies, and bursar. Having got an education themselves these young men have renounced other careers to come home and raise the next generation.

Father Anthony is in charge of education in the Diocese of Torit now; Father Taban helps refugees and preaches in Adjumani district in Uganda. Charles the Engineer is back with his family in Nairobi, but tells me he would love to return to South Sudan to construct new parish buildings and repair churches there. (Indeed, Palotaka should be a heritage site, with the beautiful old churches that were built by the Comboni Fathers restored.)

Habboba Malaria is in Juba, still working in health, and Mama Magdalene is in Juba too. I have returned to South Sudan most years since I left and hope I may continue to do so.

Managing a charity can be a demanding task. Luckily, in 2018, I met a former NGO worker, Rebecca Mallinson, who had set up a school for children from families affected by HIV or disability in Nimule, on the Nile near the border with Uganda. She introduced me to two people who were thinking of establishing a charity to help a school in Tanzania. They were willing to turn their project into an umbrella organisation. So our three projects were joined together under one registered charity, Opportunity Through Education.

It is still a headache to get anything done in South Sudan. Banks barely work outside Juba. Roads in many parts of the country, including Eastern Equatoria, are haunted by bandits and by roving army and opposition soldiers who prey on travellers. The international financial system is not set up to deal with such a situation. In 2018 the two leading money transfer organisations – Moneygram and Western Union – banned the payments I had been making to the school and students, on the basis that we might be laundering money, or else be victims of scams, or be financing terrorism. Then the Cooperative Bank froze the account, informing us that South Sudan was under sanctions and no money could be sent money there at all. I explained to them that the sanctions against South Sudan consisted of an arms embargo and financial constraints on nine specific individuals accused of human rights abuses, but it took lengthy lobbying and high-level intervention – by an activist organisation of customers set up to maintain the Cooperative Bank's ethical standards – to get the bank to unblock the account.

We continue to rely largely on informal channels to move

resources to South Sudan. So let me conclude by thanking those who help us do this, and all those who contribute to the sponsorship scheme and make it possible for us and others to continue the work of educating the next generation of South Sudanese.

Also published by City of Words

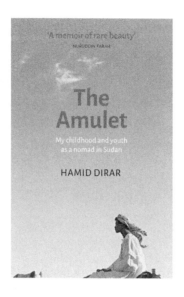

The Amulet
My childhood and youth
as a nomad in Sudan

BY HAMID DIRAR

An intimate account of childhood in a world of sheikhs and
matriarchs, camel-raiders and night-hunters. Hamid Dirar's
memoir ranges from his ancestral homeland in Nubia,
the land of rocks, to the seasonal settlements of the Butana,
the great grass plain. It is a realm of violence and beauty, with
its own laws, where the modern world is a speck
on the horizon.

ISBN 978-1-9160783-1-4

Also published by City of Words

Out of Our Hands
Encounters with the craftsmen and craftswomen of Hokkaido

BY WILLIE JONES

A personal account of the craftsmen and craftswomen of
Japan's wildest island, drawing on years of conversations
with swordsmiths, potters, painters, glass-blowers, weavers,
dyers, etchers and wood-carvers, and describing with lyrical
precision their lifelong dedication to their craft.

ISBN 978-1-9160783-3-8

Printed in Great Britain
by Amazon

76872225R00066